YOU'RE CALLER NUMBER 7, PLEASE TRY AGAIN

By

Glenn Gomez Adams

Wildebeest Publishing Company, LLC
Syracuse, NY

Do you have a story to tell? What's your animal spirit? Share it with us. #hellobeesties

You may visit the author's website at www.BaldGomez.com

Wildebeest Publishing Company, LLC

For more information about copyrights and usage, special discounts on bulk purchases, workshops, and engagements, please contact Wildebeest Publishing Company, LLC at (315) 220-0217, info@wildebeestpublishing.com, or online at www. wildebeestpublishing.com Wildebeest Publishing is dedicated to providing flexible remote work opportunities and has a presence in Syracuse, New York City, Tampa, and Denver.

Wildebeest Publishing Company, LLC, paperback First Edition [September 2025], United States of America

ISBN 978-1-958233-41-2 (paperback)
ISBN 978-1-958233-42-9 (ebook)
LLCN 2025916553

"But drink was a sovereign opium of the people, oh, an excellent opium. Although some prefer the radio, another opium of the people, a cheap one he had been using."

The Gambler, the Nun, and the Radio
Ernest Hemingway

Dedication

*To my wife, Kim, for encouraging me to write this book.
She's always been my biggest supporter. Not only did she help with this
project, but she's also helped write material for my stand-up comedy shows.
We're a good team. Kim has lovingly dealt with my alarm clock going off
at 4:00 in the morning for decades. We don't get up
early on the weekends.*

INTRODUCTION

There is a difference between *getting* up early and *being* up early. I have been in the radio business, and when I say the business, I mean the industry (an ongoing joke for longtime listeners), for over 40 years. For nearly 35 of those years, I have hosted a morning show, meaning my alarm clock has been waking me up between 3:30 and 4:00 in the morning for most of my adult life. I have always hated *getting* up early, but I have learned to love *being* up early. I've grown to enjoy the peace and quiet of the early morning hours. An old radio friend once told me that when you start doing a morning radio show, you have to say goodbye to your nighttime friends in order to make room for your new morning radio friends. My listeners have been good radio friends now for decades.

Forty or more years in any line of work produces stories and memories, hopefully good ones. That is what this book is filled with. Although there are some references to my childhood, the events and stories all took place during my radio years, a broadcasting memoir of sorts. Much like a fun road trip with friends, the stories do not necessarily go directly from point A to point B in a straight line; this collection of stories has plenty of side excursions along the way. Mostly, it's a book with fun, relatable tales I've told on the air, some involving many of the great radio people I have met over the years.

CHAPTER 1

IT'S STILL ROCK AND ROLL TO ME

Radio is fun. For example, every day for several years, we have acknowledged birthdays and other milestones on the *Gomez and Company* morning show on TK99 with "7:00 Shots," tossing back a ceremonial shot of whiskey in celebration at 7:00 in the morning. Off the top of my head, other than priests drinking wine during Sunday mass, I can't think of too many jobs where that would be considered acceptable behavior.

One of the other benefits of working in radio has always been attending lots of concerts. A common question for radio personalities to ask listeners has always been, "What was your very first concert?" It always produces great stories and memories on the air. My dad took my brothers and me to our very first concert in 1969 at the Syracuse War Memorial Auditorium. In hindsight, it was a legendary performance. Our first concert was Herb Alpert and the Tijuana Brass. We had all of Herb Alpert's albums, and they were great. I believe that every household in America in the 1960s and early 70s had a copy of the Herb Alpert album called *Whipped Cream & Other Delights*, partially because of the great music, but mainly because the album cover was the closest thing to adult entertainment that most listeners could access, and by listeners, I mean men. It wasn't quite National Geographic magazine level semi-nudity, but it was close. The photo on the cover featured a beautiful model wearing nothing but whipped cream. Head to toe. She had a rose in her left hand and was licking whipped cream from a finger on her right hand while looking seductively into the camera. What was the title of the first track on the album? I had no idea, and I didn't care. All I knew was that even if I was lactose intolerant, I wanted to jump into that pile of whipped cream.

Throughout my 40-plus years of going to shows and concerts, I have been so unbelievably fortunate to have seen the absolute legends of music perform their most recognizable songs. The most memorable of those performances for me happened on March 20th, 2015.

It was a couple of days until Spring, and I was feeling good. The weather had been decent by Syracuse standards. A March day in Central New York could mean a typical mild Spring day, or it could mean a blizzard of nearly 4 feet of snow. We've had both. I had tickets to the Syracuse Crunch hockey game the following night. The Crunch is an AHL minor league hockey team, and they are fun to watch, really a great night out.

The plan for Friday night, the 20th, was for my wife, Kim, and me to meet some friends at the Ale n' Angus Pub in downtown Syracuse for a burger and a beer at 6:00 before heading over to the War Memorial Auditorium to watch the Crunch take on the Hershey Bears. At about 4:00 on Thursday, my cell phone buzzed announcing a phone call from the radio station, and against my better judgment, I answered it. It's not that I don't enjoy my job, but often when you answer the phone during off hours, it results in more work.

"Hello," I said as I answered the call from Mimi Griswold, our longtime program director of classic rock TK99.

"Hi," she responded in a way that didn't sound like more work.

"Do you want to go to the Billy Joel concert tomorrow night in the Carrier Dome?"

I have been fortunate to have seen the legendary piano man twice before, both times inside the cavernous domed stadium on the campus of Syracuse University. On top of that, the older I get, the less I like being in crowds, especially in groups of 35 to 40 thousand. I remember the older my dad got, the earlier we left football games in order to beat the traffic. The last football game I went to before he passed away, we left, if I'm not mistaken, right after the coin toss. I totally get that.

"Well, I have plans tomorrow night to meet friends for the Crunch game," I explained.

Mimi jumped in, "Well, here's part 2 of my question. I just got off the phone with the promoter, and she asked if there was anyone at the radio station who would be available to introduce Billy on stage tomorrow night, and I thought you might enjoy that!"

Hmmm, a new wrinkle. She was right, I would enjoy that. Mainly, I would enjoy a free ticket to see Billy Joel. I tried not to sound too excited.

"Well, I guess that would be cool. Is there any chance of getting two tickets so I could bring my wife, Kim, to the concert?" Shrewd. I have always possessed the bargaining skills of a 10-year-old.

"Absolutely," Mimi answered. She added the deal sealer.

"I can also get you a parking pass to get a spot right next to the Dome." Sold! Two free tickets to see Billy Joel, a VIP parking pass, and the opportunity to introduce the legend himself in front of about 40 thousand fans. Radio has always had its perks.

Obtaining a VIP spot to park right next to the Carrier Dome in Syracuse is a BIG deal. The atmosphere inside the domed stadium was always exciting, whether it was an SU football or basketball game, a Sugar Ray Leonard boxing match, or a concert. However, actually getting to the dome can be an issue, as its location was quite possibly determined by a blindfolded game of "pin the stadium to the campus." There really is no easy way in or out of the area. Chick-fil-A often does a far better job of traffic management. I could have sold my VIP parking pass on the dark web for enough cash to actually attend Syracuse University.

I was instructed to be at a specific section of the Carrier Dome on Friday night at 6:30, meaning in order to avoid traffic hassles, we should have left our house in the northern suburbs of Syracuse sometime late afternoon…on Thursday. Obviously, that is an exaggeration, but not by much. We left our house around 5:00, thinking that would have been more than enough time to drive, park, enter the dome, find our seats, and then for me to make it to section 115 to meet the promoter.

Unlike a big football or basketball game, many concertgoers coming to the Carrier Dome were driving in from out of town. Billy Joel fans from Rochester, Utica, Watertown, and other areas of New York State and the northeast were making the trip and, therefore unfamiliar with the seemingly random traffic patterns around the Syracuse University campus, at times resembling the frozen maze that Jack Torrance tried unsuccessfully to navigate at the end of *The Shining.*

We parked in our VIP spot and made it into the packed Carrier Dome at 6:25, located our seats in the boss's suite, and made my way to the rendezvous spot at the top of section 115, just in time to meet the promoter. She led me down the stairs and behind the stage, into what would be the SU basketball team's home locker room. The area had been turned into the pre-show green room for the many technicians, stage managers, and, as it turned out, performers. She found a seat for me at the end of the table.

"I have to go find the sound tech, have a seat here next to Billy, and I'll be right back," she said.

Yes, THAT Billy. I took a seat right next to the Piano Man himself. He was surfing videos on YouTube. Billy Joel was in standard pre-concert attire for a rock star: sweatshirt, ball cap, faded jeans, and an old, comfortable pair of well-worn sneakers. He was also full of energy.

4

One thing I've noticed over the years is that successful people, whether they are rock stars, business owners, or athletes, all seem to have a great energy about them. Billy definitely had that energy. The legendary musician smiled, extended his hand, and said a quick "Hi," quickly calming my nerves. He went back to his laptop.

"I'm watching videos of The Young Rascals. I was a big fan of theirs growing up, and I want to have them open for us sometime at Madison Square Garden," he explained.

I felt like one of Billy's closest friends, and he was letting me in on some big industry secret. In reality, I probably sat with him for a couple of minutes, but it was the coolest two minutes ever.

The promoter returned and said to follow her to the backstage area to meet the sound technician, who would give me instructions before taking the stage. As I stood up to leave, Billy said, "We'll see you out there. Have fun." My nerves got the best of me. My response?

"You too." You too?! That's all I could think of?! My one moment with a music legend, and that's what came out. It was like a waiter delivering a meal at a restaurant with a friendly, "Enjoy your meal," and you unexpectedly respond with, "You too." It made no sense.

I followed the promoter out of the locker room to the enormous backstage area. Backstage at concerts is often more boring than you might think. This was not boring. This was awesome. The sound tech approached me and asked, "Are you the one who'll be making the announcement ?"

"Yes," I excitedly responded. I had quickly done the math in my head. I had done a countless number of these types of concert intros during my radio career. Usually, the stage manager hands the emcee a microphone, the emcee then heads out to a predetermined spot onstage, the sound person turns on the microphone, and then the emcee says something goofy like, "Are you ready to have a good time tonight?" Generally speaking, most people don't pay a lot of money to go somewhere with the goal of not having a good time, so as an emcee at concerts, I've never asked that question of a big crowd. Still, it's what many DJs blurt out when bringing a band onstage.

I had assumed this was to be what is referred to as a "soft intro," meaning I would introduce myself and then say something like, "Billy Joel will be coming out here to party in just a few minutes" with some enthusiasm, and then leave the stage. That type of intro seems to happen more frequently than the "hard intro," which would be more like, "Are you guys ready to rock?! Then make some noise, here's Billy Joel!" The spotlights would come up, and the music would start then and there with no delay.

The sound guy said, "Okay, you'll be standing right here at the bottom of these steps. After the second song, you'll walk up the steps, then go right to center stage and make your announcement."

Huh? Billy Joel would start his long-awaited concert in front of nearly 40,000 screaming fans, play 2 of his classic songs, and then stop playing while I walked onstage to say something? Suddenly, this sounded like a very bad plan. I would most certainly get booed by the crowd. Hell, I would boo myself at that moment.

In all my years of doing these types of things, I had never come onstage with the band after they started the concert and then made any kind of announcement.

"Are you sure this is the plan?" I asked.

"This is how Billy likes to do it," replied the sound tech.

Instructions delivered, I followed the promoter backstage again, this time to the catering area. By the time we arrived, the area was empty as the concert was about to start, with singer Gavin DeGraw opening the show.

The promoter said, "You can hang out here until Billy starts. After you get onstage, you'll have maybe 3 or 4 minutes to do your thing." I think I went pale for a moment.

"Three or four minutes for what?" I nervously asked.

"To say what you want to say about Billy. You know, it's his 7th time playing here at the Carrier Dome and they're raising an honorary number 7 jersey to the roof to honor the occasion," she replied.

I was aware of the jersey celebration, but I assumed that would take all of 30 seconds. What the hell was I supposed to talk about for three or four minutes?

As she turned to leave, she added, "Oh, by the way, Billy wants to know how you would like him to introduce you?"

"I was just going to say something like, 'Welcome to the Carrier Dome, here's Billy Joel,'" I said. She shook her head.

"No, Billy is going to introduce YOU and bring you up on stage with him." I blinked nervously for a moment, and as we say on the radio, experienced dead air. Our radio station has a silence alarm that goes off after seven seconds of dead air. If I had been equipped with one, it would have been buzzing right then and there.

"Oh," I stammered. "He can just say, here's Gomez from TK99."

I figured I would make it easy for him. Afterward, I thought of all the things I should have had him say. "He was a former running back with the Ottawa Rough Riders of the CFL, a member of the US Olympic 4-man bobsled team, and a one-time shuttle astronaut. Would you please welcome Gomez!"

She left me alone in the catering area with my thoughts and a giant platter of chocolate chip cookies. Sometimes the backstage catering area at concerts has a veggie tray and a keg of beer. Sometimes it's a tray of tiny sandwiches like in *Spinal Tap*. Sometimes it's just chips and dips and a cooler filled with bottled water. Billy Joel had barbeque, cornbread, delicious sides, desserts, and a giant tray of chocolate chip cookies. For a moment, my inner fat guy took over, and I instinctively grabbed a huge cookie. Even while I was eating it, I was wondering how to grab a couple more and stash them in my pockets for later.

Then I heard Gavin DeGraw and his band start. The show had begun, and according to the promoter, I had to speak for 3 or 4 minutes in front of some 40 thousand fans about the great Billy Joel after he had introduced me onstage. I sat down at one of the long, empty tables and started to scribble out a few notes. It was his record 7th appearance in the Carrier Dome, his daughter Alexa had performed at our annual local food festival, The Taste of Syracuse, he had donated a big chunk of cash to the Syracuse University school of music, and I'd been playing his music on the radio for over 35 years. As Gavin DeGraw entertained the crowd, my little talk was coming together.

Although I was starting to get nervous, I had already scored a big win. The fact that Billy Joel was the one who would introduce me probably minimized the chance of being booed. Think of any-time you've been to a baseball game and the mayor, or a senator, or any politician comes out to throw out the first pitch. "Booooo!" If I were sitting in the dome and Billy Joel was rocking away, and then suddenly the show came to a halt as somebody got onstage and started yakking away, I would boo as well.

I had outlined my talk and at first thought I would keep the notes in my pocket in case I got nervous, but then I thought screw it. If Billy Joel had confidence in me on this night, then I was going onstage without notes.

Gavin DeGraw finished his opening set, and the stage was be-ing readied for Billy Joel. The promoter came back to the catering area to get me.

"It's time," she said. "I'll bring you to the backstage spot where you'll wait until Billy introduces you and calls you onstage." Gulp. I instantly forgot everything I was planning to say to the crowd. And of course, I had thrown away my notes.

I stood up, grabbed another cookie from the tray, and fol-lowed. We walked through the long hallway that passes the door to the SU home locker room where I had met Billy earlier, turned a hard right, and then through the short tunnel from which leg-endary head coach Jim Boeheim and the Syracuse Orange bas-ketball team emerged to run onto the basketball court. I thought about the late, great SU basketball legend "Pearl" Washington run-ning down the same tunnel and hallway moments after hitting a game-winning half-court shot to beat Boston College many years before. I followed her to the stage manager's spot, right next to one of the several light and sound boards set up at the base of the short staircase that led up to the stage.

Billy Joel and his amazing band had started the show, the crowd was on its feet, and the dome was rocking. I stood there taking it all in when I noticed a copy of the setlist taped up on the soundboard. According to a handwritten note on the list, the "DJ intro" would take place after the second song. There it was in print. Two songs in, and I would take the stage. Halfway through the second song, "Pressure," the butterflies kicked into high gear. The Piano Man had certainly picked the right song for the occasion. On a scale of nervousness for guys, it was right up there somewhere between taking a driver's license road test and seeing rotating red lights in the rear view mirror.

I was standing at the bottom of the stairs that led up to the stage and taking deep breaths. My heart was beating like I had just completed the 10-mile Mountain Goat Run through the streets of Syracuse. I remember thinking, "I could be two beers into a hockey game right now."

In reality, there was no place I would have rather been at that exact moment of my life, as I have learned that there is no growth in comfort. The most memorable moments of life have some degree of excitement, nerves, purpose, or uneasiness. For me, this was one of those moments.

"Pressure" ended, and the Carrier Dome crowd burst into screams and applause. Billy Joel and his dynamic band were on fire and rocking the arena. I thought the last thing this crowd wanted to see or hear was a local radio DJ talking between songs and bringing the smoking hot concert to a complete halt. Cue Gomez. As the crowd calmed down, Billy Joel leaned into his piano-mounted microphone for his introduction.

"I'd like to bring up Gomez from TK99."

The stage manager handed me a wireless microphone and said, "It's hot. Walk out to the center mic stand and start talking."

I took one last deep breath and jogged up the stairs to the stage, walked past Billy and his piano to my left, and his band to my right. As I had hoped, the fact that Billy is the one who introduced me to the crowd was definitely an asset. People applauded, but primarily because he had done the introduction. Had I stopped the concert to introduce myself, I would have been booed like Yoko Ono at a Beatles concert.

I looked out at some 40 thousand fans. The stage lights were bright, and I could really only see the people in the first few rows, and the silhouettes of fans way back and directly opposite the stage, who were standing in front of the lighted concourse. I thought I should try to get the crowd on my side, so I blurted into the microphone the first thing that came to my mind.

"That just became the coolest thing that had ever happened to me," which brought a few applause and some cheers.

Billy added, "You should get out more," which drew some laughter from the crowd. I was now having somewhat of a conversation with Billy Joel in front of a sold-out stadium! It really was the coolest thing that had ever happened to me.

I was wearing a leather jacket, and my cell phone was in the inside breast pocket. As I continued to speak, I could feel the phone buzzing and vibrating, and it continued to do so the entire time I was onstage. Friends and coworkers were texting me and sending pictures they had just taken. It was truly one of the most exciting moments of my life, and definitely the most memorable moment in my years in the radio business.

I'm not even sure of exactly what I said over the next few minutes. I know I congratulated him on his record seventh appearance in the Carrier Dome. I had also mentioned his daughter's appearance in Syracuse and thanked him for his generous donation to the SU School of Music. Then, I helped cheer on the crowd as his number seven jersey was raised to the rafters of the stadium. As I turned to leave the stage, Billy smiled my way, gave me a thumbs up, and mouthed the words "thank you." I smiled back and returned the thumbs up as I walked across the stage and down the stairs.

As I walked up the stairs to join my wife and coworkers in the boss's suite to enjoy the rest of the concert, I remember thinking, if today were my last day in the radio business, I would be happy. I couldn't imagine topping that experience. That was in 2015, and it is still a true statement, even after over 40 years behind the microphone.

So, how did I get to share the stage with Billy Joel? The incredible journey to that moment took over 4 decades. Let me hit the rewind button and explain.

CHAPTER 2

ATTICA WAITING

I was an honors graduate from Marcellus Senior High School in 1978. I also once moved, with the help of several of my friends, the principal's Volkswagen from the teacher's parking lot to the front doorway of the high school. That pretty much explains how I started out as a chemical engineering student at SUNY Buffalo and ended up with a 40-plus-year career in radio. Without getting too much into the specifics, while in Buffalo, I discovered beer and music. At that time in Western New York, there was a beer called Goebel. In 1978, Goebel beer cost, no lie, $3.88. Not for a six pack, but for a case. My roommate Paul and I would routinely split a case of Goebel beer in our dorm room…and then go out. We did that way too often, but it was a blast. Anyone in my age group can remember going out to the bars until last call, then maybe out for breakfast, getting home at 3:00 in the morning, and then waking up feeling great at 6:00 to go to work, often wearing the same clothes from the night before. Now, if I eat ice cream after 7:00 in the evening, it's going to be a long night.

Another activity that I loved while at the University of Buffalo, or UB, was playing my trombone. The trombone is an awesome instrument as it is one of the brass backbones of any jazz or concert band. The great trombonists are true virtuosos who can make the instrument sing. You can also make great fart noises with it. I was more of the latter.

Looking back, maybe I should have learned to play the guitar or the piano. I started playing the trombone in the third grade and continued to play through college. At parties, people are always asking guitar players or pianists to play some great old Rolling Stones tunes or holiday music. I have never been to a party where someone said, "Hey Glenn, why don't you go get your old trombone and belt out the lower, bass clef notes of a dixieland classic?"

I played in three different bands in Buffalo: the SUNY Buffalo Concert Band, the Canisius College Jazz Band, and the Daemen College Big Band. It was so much fun. The jazz band and the big band actually got paid, often in beer, to play gigs. At that time, Buffalo was a great jazz city. The old Tralfamadore Cafe on Main Street and Fillmore Avenue was a legendary jazz and R&B venue. And I once saw the Buffalo-based jazz group Spirogyra perform at the Record Theater store on Main Street. They were fantastic. I remember thinking if they ever needed a trombone player who could make awesome fart noises on the horn, I was their guy.

One night at a rehearsal in the spring of 1979 with the Daemen College big band, the director had an announcement.

"Hey guys, listen up, I have some great news. We have a gig coming up next month, and it's a paying gig! We're going to get $200 to play for an hour. It's a bit of a drive, so I'll rent a van for us. Oh, and don't forget to bring your driver's license." Driver's license? We assumed the gig must be at a bar or club. The legal drinking age in New York State in 1979 was 18, so we all figured we would be getting proofed at the door before the show.

"That's cool," I said enthusiastically, adding, "What's the name of the bar for the gig? Is it the Tralf? Or the Brickyard Bar?" mentioning a few of Buffalo's famous jazz spots.

"Not quite," the band director replied. "We're playing Attica." I had never heard of that venue, so I piped up.

"You mean there's a bar called Attica?" I remember thinking, *Who would name a bar after the site of a horrible prison riot?*

"It's not a bar called Attica," the director answered. "We're actually playing a gig inside the Attica Correctional Facility."

The disturbing Attica prison riots took place only 8 years before, and were currently being taught in high school history classes, and now we had a gig booked there.

The band director needed our driver's licenses to call ahead to Attica prison to let them know who was in our band, so they could do a background check and see if any of us had any relatives who were inmates, just in case we were thinking of smuggling in nail files or porn. I have no idea what people actually try to sneak into prisons, but in movies, it's almost always nail files baked inside a cake. I've always assumed the nail files were used to pick locks and not give manicures. And I only thought porn because, well, it's prison. And I was only mildly concerned about another riot.

In reality, there is precisely zero chance of me surviving a prison fight or riot. If I had ever appeared in a movie about prison riots, I would be one of the nameless inmates with no dialogue, probably named in the credits as "dead prisoner number 1." I would definitely be the first guy down.

On the day of the show, the band director rented a van to take us from Daemen College in Buffalo to the Attica Correctional Facility, a distance of 35 miles or so. We joked along the way, but they were the nervous kind of jokes that aren't really that funny, eliciting the kind of laughs that aren't actual laughs, like dark humor at a funeral.

The jokes completely stopped when the van pulled into the parking lot of the Attica prison at around 1:00. The band director parked the van, and we all nervously got out, grabbed our instruments, and walked single file as instructed into the front doors of Attica prison. Gulp. We entered a receiving area where we had to sign in, produce our driver's licenses, and answer a few questions.

For example, "How many cigarettes would you be able to bet on the Super Bowl?" At least that's what I thought they might ask.

All of my knowledge of the prison system is what I had seen in movies, meaning it was probably all wrong. For instance, I had no idea if license plates were actually made in prisons, but if they were, I agree with those who have always felt sorry for inmates of the New Hampshire prison system who were forced to make license plates with their state slogan, "Live Free or Die."

We then had to bring our instruments over to a large table where Attica guards opened and searched all of our instruments, as well as the cases that contained them, for any contraband we may have been trying to sneak into the prison. As a kid, I once tried to fit my younger brother Michael into my trombone case, and as I recall, it was close, so I totally understood their concern.

The Attica prison gates opened and closed like the airlocks on the USS Enterprise on *Star Trek*. We walked in silence through the prison yard and into another building.

The door to an auditorium opened, and we were led in by prison trustees happy to see us. At least I believed they were trustees. Again, all I knew up to that point about prison life and the vernacular came from Hollywood. These guys were friendly, courteous, and had clearly been in Attica for quite some time. As I have said many times on my radio show, there are many questions in life that I'm glad I don't know the answers to, and one of them would be, "How would I look after spending several years in a maximum security prison?"

We brought our instrument cases to the rear of the stage, where tables and chairs had been set up for our lunch. Yes indeed, we were about to have lunch at Attica prison. With actual Attica prisoners. And Attica food. Lunch came as a complete surprise to us. What would they possibly serve us? Soup? Creamed corn? Cold baked beans?

As it turned out, cheese sandwiches were on the menu that day. And I mean just one slice of nearly stale cheese with the edges turning brown, in between 2 slices of old bread, in a state of stale-ness somewhere between crusty hard and moldy penicillin. And no condiments. An inmate, I would guess to be in his mid-40s, handed me the cheese sandwich.

"Enjoy," he added with a smile.

I took a bite, and it actually compared favorably to a few of the meals served in college dining halls. All of us in the band were college students accustomed to eating everything from gas station burritos to mac and cheese, to expired lunch meats, and worse.

I returned the smile and said, "Thanks," to the inmate who provided my lunch. I had no idea who he was or what he was convicted of to be sent to serve his time in Attica. He seemed like a nice guy, and being given the trust to be let out of his cell to make sandwiches and serve them to a bunch of college kids was a big deal for him.

Then, the doors to the auditorium opened. One by one, with plenty of guards to accompany them, the inmates of Attica Correctional Facility filed into the large room and took their seats following the specific directions being given to them.

"Please move all the way down the row without skipping any seats. Thank you." The verbal instructions were coming over the public address system.

The inmates were in what I would consider to be a pretty good mood. Having never been incarcerated, I have no clue as to what constitutes a good mood, but to me, it looked like they were in one. The inmates were seated, lunch had been eaten, our instruments were warmed up, we were ready to go.

The band director took his spot at the front of the stage, facing us with his back to the audience. He took a big breath, turned to face the large crowd, and spoke.

"Thank you for inviting us to play for you today, and we're all happy to be here. Our first song for you this afternoon is a classic big band number called 'Waiting.'"

The director quickly realized the painful irony of the song

selection as he turned back around to face us. He looked as though he had just seen the cops in the rearview mirror. To call the ensuing moment of silence "awkward" would be like calling that horrible stuff they use in nail salons "aromatic." We were going to play a song for prison inmates called "Waiting." After a few seconds that seemed much longer, an inmate in about the 4th row and left of the center aisle broke the uncomfortable silence.

"Waitin'?" he asked loudly. "Who's waitin'? Anyone here waitin'?"

"Hey, Ray, are you waitin'?" His friend Ray yelled back to him.

"I ain't waitin', I got all the time in the world."

The exchange prompted much-needed laughter. It was an unbelievable icebreaker and brought immediate relief to the band. I've never had to wait for the results of an STD test, but I imagine the relief of a negative result would be the same.

The band director raised his baton, and we played "Waiting" and the rest of our program. I'd like to say it was our best concert ever, but it wasn't. By the time we had settled into a groove after shaking off the nerves and anxiety, the inmates began to stand up and file out, literally in the middle of a song. Over the music, we could hear the announcements through the public address system directing inmates to stand and exit the auditorium by their cell block. We lost 20 or 30 inmates at a time until the room was empty. After the final notes echoed from our last song, we quickly put our instruments back in their cases and returned through the prison yard, back to the main reception area. The director collected our pay for the performance, and we all hopped back in the van and made the trip back to Buffalo. As I recall, we were paid two hundred dollars for the show. Rather than split it up 12 or 13 ways for each band member, we pooled the cash and spent it on a party of beer and wings. This is why musicians often live in vans.

I sometimes think about that day, and what became of the inmates who watched the Daemen College Jazz Band concert at the Attica Correctional Facility in the spring of 1979. Did our little show have any impact on any of them? And perhaps most importantly, could someone please deliver fresh cheese to Attica prison?!

I returned to the UB campus in the fall of 1979 for my sophomore semester, refreshed and ready for round two of my scheduled 4-round battle with the engineering program. SUNY Buffalo is a very large university, often with class sizes that resemble national Amway meetings. The chemistry class I took as a freshman had more students in it than my entire graduating class from Marcellus High School, and definitely more chemicals. My roommates also took chemistry, and I believe they were there to learn how to make their own supplies for recreational purposes. I took engineering, they took medicine. Literally.

I remember going to one specific house party on Minnesota Avenue near the Main Street campus with my roommates. Like every college party, the place was jam-packed and the beers were flowing. I lost track of my roommates for an hour or so, and the next time I saw them, they were "experimenting." Some guy they had just met, named Ross from Long Island, had introduced them to a new, recreational hallucinogen. They asked me if I wanted to try it with them, and I kindly declined. They then consumed what I guess was considered more than the recommended dosage. Although I am not a doctor, I assumed this was not the prescribed amount of the hallucinogen because this party was on a Saturday, and I did not see them again until the following Wednesday. To nobody's surprise, they majored in pharmacology.

By the midway point of the fall semester of my sophomore year, my grades were marginal at best. I also made the mistake of taking a scuba diving class that would meet every Saturday morning at 9:00. The class was all guys, and for the most part, we would often arrive in various stages of hangover, toss all of our scuba gear into the deep end of the pool, jump in, and sit motionless at the bottom of the pool breathing pure oxygen. Therapeutic, perhaps, but ultimately not very helpful. Maybe it was the hangover, perhaps the pure oxygen, or quite possibly the 46 I received on a recent Physics test, but on one of those Saturday mornings at the bottom of the pool in the fall of 1979, I decided that engineering was not going to happen for me. I limped across the finish line of that semester with barely passing grades and moved back to Marcellus.

After the Christmas holiday break, I enrolled in classes at my beloved Onondaga Community College, conveniently located about 6 miles from my parents' house, and about 3 miles from the Poor House West, home of 2-dollar pitchers of lukewarm beer and basically everyone I had ever known. For those who never had the opportunity to experience the Poor House West, it had the aroma of stale beer, sweat, hormones, along with the faint scent of disappointment. At that moment, I had no idea what I wanted to do, or to what program I wanted to apply, I just knew that if I didn't register for classes somewhere, I probably would not have returned to college and would have started working somewhere, quite possibly the Poor House West.

The first week of classes at OCC was pretty basic college courses. English, psychology, a science elective, etc. Sometime during that week, I bumped into the only person I knew on campus, a high school friend named Don. Don was an eclectic guy, a big fan of the counterculture writer Hunter S. Thompson, and had a uniquely bizarre sense of humor. He had that kind of humor that only a few people got, but he didn't care. He had a lot to say about pretty much everything, and he had a weekly show on the college radio station. I started hanging around Don and the radio station, and that's when I first thought of broadcasting as something I wanted to pursue as a career. Shortly after, I officially enrolled in the Radio/Television department and began taking the necessary classes that would point me in the direction of a career in radio.

There were times over the years when I thought perhaps I should have been on another path. For example, when my first full-time job in my chosen profession paid less than the guy who filled the soap dispenser in the men's room. But was he having as much fun as I was? Based on the aroma of the not-yet-legal marijuana on his clothes, I would guess that he was probably having more fun than I was.

What I mainly learned from my classes at OCC was that I enjoyed the creative process of radio more than the medium itself. Looking back over the years, radio was, and continues to be, a means to an end. For me, radio has been a way to earn a living doing something innovative. In hindsight, I suppose I could have enjoyed a career as a writer, performer, graphic artist, or whatever as long as it allowed for creativity. That is the part that drew me to a career in radio. It was, and still is, a creative outlet.

Radio is also never boring; every day is different. Over my 40-plus years behind the microphone, I have met some incredible people and done some amazing things that I never would have done had I ended up somewhere as a chemical engineer. Of course, I would probably have had better benefits and an alarm clock set for 6:30 AM instead of 3:50 AM, but how boring would that have been? I would have been a well-rested engineer with no cool stories to tell.

CHAPTER 3

EARLY RADIO WAVES

When I was growing up in the 1960s and 1970s, entertainment options were limited. There was television featuring three main channels with the major networks ABC, NBC, and CBS. There was the Public Broadcasting Station, but the reception was spotty at best at our house in Marcellus, New York. We could occasionally pick up the NBC affiliate from Utica. And every now and then, the fuzzy picture from a Canadian TV station was clear enough to see some of the shows, even the more adult programming. My friend, Mike, who lived down the road, would sometimes call to say, "The Canadian station is coming in really clear tonight!" I would hop on my chopper bicycle with a banana seat and ride to his house to watch what we considered to be soft porn, but in reality was probably just a late-night Canadian soap opera.

Movie theaters were another entertainment option. Present-day movie theater chains have beautiful theaters offering all of the latest amenities, and by that, I mean high-priced tickets and really expensive snacks. Looking through the glass snack case, trying to choose a candy bar at a modern, fancy movie theater feels like shopping for jewelry. I once paid 12 dollars for a new watch from the jewelry case at a K-Mart, and 21 dollars for Twizzlers and popcorn from the snack case at a movie theater. I've always preferred the smaller, independent family-owned movie theaters that offer sticky floors, reasonably priced Raisinettes, and movies that are "pretty current."

Of course, there were the classic kids' games that provided hours of entertainment. For example, long before video games and PlayStations, we would play games like hide and seek. In this game, one kid was selected to close his or her eyes, count to 10 while every other kid would find a hiding spot, and just sit there and wait. The kid with his or her eyes closed would then call out something like, "Ready or not, here I come," and then try to find everyone. The job of those hiding was to find a spot to hide, and be as quiet as possible for as long as possible. This game was clearly invented by a mom.

There have always been live performance entertainment options. Theater was always available, but for kids, that wasn't really high on the list of priorities. Boys began to develop interest in theater right around the time when they realized that girls had developed an interest in theater. I can't speak for all guys, but most of my friends who auditioned for parts in plays and musicals did so to meet girls. Plus, growing up in a large family, buying tickets to things like live performances was not in the budget.

The only other real entertainment option was radio. Radio was free, interactive, and immediate. For example, radio was the first place we learned about school closings. On bad-weather mornings during the long winter months in the northeast, sitting by the radio waiting to hear if your school was closed was high drama at its finest. As mentioned, I grew up in Marcellus, so alphabetically we had to wait to hear, "Jordan Elbridge, Lafayette, Lyncourt, Madison," etc., until the radio announcer would say "Marcellus." For a kid during that time period, hearing your school closed on the radio was about the greatest feeling in the world. Radio guys were rock stars.

For anyone who took the school bus to school every morning, the radio was the main source of entertainment, unless a kid puked and the driver had to stop the bus and sprinkle the magic sawdust on the floor. Taking the school bus in the 1970s was much different than it is today. For example, if you've ever been stuck behind a school bus, you quickly learn that the driver is not allowed to let a kid off the bus in front of his or her house unless a parent or guardian is home and comes out to meet them. This process often takes so long that, on one occasion, while waiting behind a stopped school bus in our neighborhood, by the time the driver could open the school bus door to let the second-grade student off the bus, the kid was in the third grade. At least, that's how long it felt. When I was that age, the driver would not only let you off the bus, he would often let you off the bus at your friend's house, a corner store, or wherever. The school bus was our form of public transportation.

On the school bus, you basically listened to whatever the bus driver was listening to. In my case, the school bus driver that we had pretty much all the way from middle school to high school listened to one of the "top 40" radio stations in Syracuse, usually preferring the popular "Rick and Ron" morning show. The ride from the end of our driveway to the drop-off at school took about 25 minutes or so, giving us plenty of time to hear the antics and song parodies of the highly rated radio show. Rick and Ron were funny, likable, a little goofy, and perfect for morning radio in the 1970s. That was the first time I can remember thinking about how much fun it must be working at a radio station.

But the very first time I can recall actually paying close attention to radio, and being fascinated by it, was on March 8th, 1971. That was the date of the first heavyweight fight between Muhammad Ali and "Smokin'" Joe Frazier. The championship bout was held at Madison Square Garden in New York City. The fight had been promoted for months, and to this day, remains one of the most anticipated sporting events in history. There were only two ways to see the fight. You either bought a ticket and saw it in person at MSG, or you paid for a local "pay-per-view" event at a local movie theater. One of the local theaters that showed the fight LIVE was the Landmark Theater in downtown Syracuse. The huge fight drew a crowd of close to 3,000 fans who each paid $12.50, or to put it into perspective, in today's money, the equivalent of two cups of coffee at Starbucks. I remember wanting to join the sold-out crowd at the Landmark to watch the fight, but two things prevented me from attending.

One was the cost. According to the inflation calculator on the internet, $12.50 in 1971 would be worth a little over $91.00 today, or about the equivalent of a can of Lysol during the pandemic. And as we all know, you can't put anything on the internet if it isn't true.

The second obstacle to going to the Landmark Theater to watch the Ali vs. Frazier fight was that I couldn't get a ride to downtown Syracuse. Although I had learned how to drive by navigating my uncle Ernie's old jeep through the fields of my grandmother's farm in the Adirondack Mountains the previous summer, in March of 1971, I was, in fact, 11 years old. I had some friends in my neighborhood, who were not much older than me, offer to drive me downtown for the fight. We'll just say that many laws regarding motor vehicles in rural areas in the 1970s were treated more like good suggestions. A 13-year-old behind the wheel of a Chevy Nova dropping off an unaccompanied 11-year-old at a pay-per-view boxing match in 1971 may not have raised an eyebrow. Needless to say, I did not make it to the Landmark Theater.

The only other option was radio. A local station was providing LIVE updates between the rounds of the match. I had a small transistor radio with an earplug, and I listened to the fight updates all night long. It was fascinating. I don't remember the name of the broadcaster who was providing the updates, but I remember closing my eyes and picturing what he was describing in between the rounds at Madison Square Garden. I could "see" the crowd, "smell" the beer, and "feel" the electricity. I felt like I was there. With his voice, the broadcaster transported me to a different world that I could sense and be a part of. It was an unbelievable couple of hours of entertainment.

After the "Fight of the Century," I began to pay closer attention to radio. At night, after I went to bed, I would turn on my little transistor radio and slowly scroll the circular tuning dial to see what faraway radio stations I could listen to after dark. I picked up "The Big One," 700 WLW in Cincinnati and listened to the late-night DJ play country music requests for the truckers who were listening in from highways all around the Midwest and beyond. I became a St. Louis Cardinals baseball fan when I started tuning in broadcasts of their games on 1120 KMOX, with legendary announcer Jack Buck at the microphone. That is also why my Little League baseball mitt was a Bob Gibson model, emblazoned with the signature of the legendary Hall of Fame pitcher. I would listen to the nighttime personalities on WNBC in New York City, WBZ in Boston, WLS in Chicago, and countless others. My little transistor radio, powered by a 9-volt battery, provided me with hour upon hour of entertainment.

As much as I became a devoted listener and fan of radio as a medium, I still never thought of broadcasting as a career. I had my favorite local stations and DJs. In the early 1970s, I was a huge fan of Syracuse radio station 620AM WHEN, known as "The Entertainer." The station was known for big personalities and even bigger radio promotions. In 1974, WHEN had a promotion called "WHEN has gone bananas," and one of the DJs lived about 40 feet above the street in a giant banana for about a week. The on-air personalities would randomly call people on the air, and someone would have to answer their phone by saying, "WHEN's gone bananas" to win the grand prize and let the DJ out of the giant banana. It might not sound that entertaining by today's standards, but in 1974, it was a monster promotion that had people talking, and I still remember it all these years later.

In the summer of 1977, the great comedian Steve Martin was red hot from his Saturday Night Live appearances and comedy albums, and he was on tour with a scheduled performance at the Grandstand at the New York State Fair, and WHEN was giving away tickets. I happened to walk into our kitchen, and the radio was on as the DJ cracked open his microphone.

"Call in right now, and whoever does the best impression of Steve Martin will win a pair of tickets to his State Fair show!"

I ran to the phone and dialed up the number, and about 30 seconds later, I was LIVE on the air with the DJ! For my impression, I went with Steve Martin's Czechoslovakian character from the "Two Wild and Crazy Guys" skit from Saturday Night Live, Georg Festrunk. When the DJ said, "Let's hear it," I went right into my impression.

"How many astro sign medallions can YOU wear? Next time, try five of them!" in my best Festrunk brother accent. Complete silliness, but pretty much a direct quote from one of the Festrunk brothers' SNL segments.

I was a little nervous, but it was good enough to win. Score! Not only did I get to bring my friend Mike, the same friend who would call me to ride my bike to his house to watch the risque Canadian soap operas, to see Steve Martin, but it marked the first time I was actually on the radio. My brother Gary was listening and heard it, and that was pretty cool.

While people still tune into radio, especially local radio, I believe people had a different connection with the medium a few years back. For example, today, anyone can download or stream almost any song they want to hear, whenever they want to listen to it. It literally takes a few seconds to find a song and play it. When you wanted to hear a song pre-internet, you had to call your favorite DJ on your favorite music radio station, be thrilled if he or she actually picked up the phone, even more excited when they asked what song you wanted to hear, and then said something like, "I'll try to get that one on for you." And you believed it. Your favorite DJ would never lie to you.

After you hung up the phone, you went over to the radio in your bedroom, or kitchen, or family room, or wherever you listened, and you waited. And waited. And waited some more. Hopefully, the first few notes of your song came blaring out of your radio, and if you were lucky, the DJ said your name! For a teenager, there was nothing more exciting than that feeling, even slightly ahead of hearing that your school was closed for the day. An added bonus would have been if you had a sound system with a cassette player, and you had a blank cassette in the tape compartment, and were able to hit the record button at just the right time to get a clean copy of the tune. Getting a song recorded by this method was an early example of how we "stuck it to the man." Free music. It took effort, patience, and a little luck. But oh man, what a cherished accomplishment.

Finding your favorite song now takes little more than a verbal request of a smart speaker or a few clicks on your smartphone. Although you get to hear your song, there's little invested in the process. I've always believed that it offers a different connection to music and radio.

That was pretty much my relationship with radio at that point in my life. Although I was fascinated with tuning into faraway stations at night and listening to my favorite local DJs of the time, it never dawned on me to make a career of it. I wasn't a true "radio nerd" like so many of my longtime radio friends. I have worked with guys who were so into radio as kids, they built their own radio stations in their parents' basements and spare rooms. Some of these little homemade pirate radio stations were pretty good and better equipped than some actual commercial radio stations I have worked at over the years. These guys would hang around real radio stations, see what equipment they were throwing out, and then grab it to bring home. They would get their hands on a "crystal radio kit" from a store like Radio Shack to be able to broadcast their station, usually just a small area within a mile or so from their house. On a nerd scale, these guys were somewhere between a middle school earth science teacher and Jeffrey Dahmer. They could have gone either way.

Since I didn't have the radio nerd gene, I assumed that I should take my decent math and science grades to college and study chemical engineering; that failed experiment that lasted three semesters at the University of Buffalo. Don't get me wrong, SUNY Buffalo is a fine University with a great engineering school. It is also very close to lots and lots of bars. Without getting into too many details, I once went out with some friends and woke up under a picnic table on the campus of Buffalo State College, which, although sounds similar, is in fact a completely different college. The details of that night remain a mystery.

CHAPTER 4

SNAKES!

Radio is to entertainment what haggis is to fine Scottish cuisine. At least, that has always been the perception. I have always laughed at Hollywood's depiction of radio DJs, whether it was Harry Shearer's "Handsome Dan" in *Wayne's World 2,* or Pawnee, Indiana's "Crazy Ira and the Douche," as portrayed by Matt Besser and Nick Kroll in the comedy series *Parks and Recreation.* While over-the-top portrayals are exaggerations of radio people, the performances are often not far off target. I find these movies and television shows featuring fictional radio stations and DJs entertaining in the way I assume NASCAR drivers laugh at Will Ferrell's Ricky Bobby in *Talladega Nights,* or the way golfers still love *Caddyshack.* The depictions are based on love. I hope.

Anyone and everyone who has been in radio for any length of time has at least one story of working at a radio station that seemed like one of these fictional broadcast facilities. My very first real radio job was in Herkimer, New York, at a small AM station with the call letters WRMV, which stood for "Radio of the Mohawk Valley." (For geographic reference, the Mohawk Valley is a beautiful area located between the Adirondack Mountains and the Catskill Mountains. From Syracuse, you just head east on the New

York State Thruway, and set your cruise control and GPS...to the late 1950s. I say that with love.)

The radio station shared space with an insurance company in a small, one-story building in downtown Herkimer. Herkimer is a charming little town with a vibrant Main Street, a good diner, blue-collar bars, and lots of hard-working people not afraid to tell it like it is. It would be the perfect setting for a Hallmark Christmas movie if it were going to air on HBO. It was my first radio job and my first time living on my own. The gig didn't pay well at all, not much more than minimum wage, but I didn't care. It got me on the radio, and it was the start of my broadcasting career.

On my first day on the job, I recorded a commercial for a local furniture store, and I looked up when it was going to air on 1420 WRMV. The first airing of the spot was scheduled at 10:20 the next morning. I can remember being in my little $195-a-month apartment on King Street the next morning, turning on my K-Mart stereo system, tuning in 1420 AM, then sitting on my bed waiting for the 30-second commercial to air. I remember the anticipation and then the excitement of hearing my voice on a real, commercial radio station! It was the coolest thing ever. I was so thrilled that I treated myself to the $6.99 dinner at the Ponderosa Steak House.

The job in Herkimer wasn't the most challenging; in fact, it eventually became boring. The on-air shift was known as "live-assist automation," meaning I could pre-record the news and other on-air segments, and just program them into the automation system. After I got the hang of it, the job was little more than babysitting for a few hours. It got to the point where I could get everything all set, wait until the rest of the staff had gone home for the day, and then sneak out of the building through a back window. I would drive to a few of the bars in the evening, occasionally going out to my car and turning on the radio station to make sure it was still on the air.

The most exciting thing that happened was being asked if I

wanted to be the station's assistant engineer for an extra $25 a paycheck, which, after taxes, totaled less than a daily cup of coffee. They drove a hard bargain. I said, "Sure." The added responsibilities mainly consisted of weekly trips to take meter readings at the transmitter site, conveniently located in a nearby swamp.

I started to wonder if it was time to move on. It should have been a sign when my $25 Christmas bonus check bounced. That's radio. Somehow, I managed to hang in there until late spring of 1982, when I finally decided to leave the radio station, but through the front door. Other than the bounced Christmas bonus check, it was not a bad little radio station for a first radio job. However, the next radio station was one of those that still gets talked about to this day.

I answered the ad for the overnight position at WKFM in Fulton, New York, and was invited to come in for an interview at the radio station in the very fancy-sounding "Radio Park" broadcast facility. I wore my one suit and my dad's London Fog overcoat, looking more like a member of Scotland Yard than a radio DJ. This was obviously way before GPS or Google Maps, so I just followed the instructions given to me on how to get to Radio Park. It was the exact opposite of fancy. I drove by the building, thinking this can't be the place. It was a small, concrete bunker-looking building at the end of a short dirt road in a swamp, the kind of location investigated on episodes of *Forensic Files*.

I parked my 1973 Ford Gran Torino next to three other cars of similar age, each with generous amounts of rust, bird poop, and not a complete set of tires between them that would have passed inspection. Radio people. My people. And definitely not from sales. I walked into the building and was instantly met by Brian Richards, Gary Dunes, and the program director, John Carucci. After a few pleasantries and a quick tour of the studios, I sat down with John to talk about the job and my experience.

"You're hired."

That should have been a sign right there. The shortest job

31

interview ever, and I was offered the job. I would be doing the over-night show. Back in the day, an on-air shift was a 6-day work week. I would work Sunday through Thursday night from midnight to 6:00 AM, and my Saturday evening shift would be from 6:00 to midnight.

We were a thin staff with just four full-timers and two part-timers. Brian did the morning shift from 6:00 AM until noon. John handled afternoons from noon until 6:00 PM. Gary was the nighttime jock from 6:00 until midnight, and then I took over for the overnight shift. Jim Reith and Bryan Rubenau were the capable part-timers. This was 1983, so the radio station was totally old school, playing records and albums on turntables, drinking horrible coffee from an ancient coffee maker, talking to the par-tiers and insomniacs who called the station throughout the night, and checking the old Associated Press wire machine for news and weather updates. I can still hear that old ticker, and I miss that sound.

The old studio in the swamp had one bathroom, a single-seater that was right in the on-air studio. I mean, it was right there, less than three steps from the studio microphone. If someone was in there and flushed the toilet while the mic was on, it could be heard on the radio, which was awesome. I can remember arriving for my shift shortly before midnight and having Gary flush the toilet with the microphone on while I sat out in my car to listen to it on the radio. It was radio magic, and by that, I mean if the program direc-tor heard it, we both would have been in trouble.

I started that job in the spring of 1983 and worked through the hot summer. The building was neither air-conditioned nor heated. The facility was warmed in the winter months from the heat gener-ated by the transmitter, which was also in the same building. Quite honestly, I don't even know if that setup was built to code. A duct was attached from the transmitter and vented through the ceiling and into the studio. Again, I don't know if that was legal, or healthy for that matter, but I can tell you it didn't throw off very much heat.

During the one winter I worked there, I can remember having to wear a hat and gloves in the studio all night long.

In the summer, the building was flat-out hot with zero ventilation. It was in a swamp, meaning the facility came fully equipped with spiders, mosquitoes, frogs, mice, and snakes. Although they are annoying, I can deal with mosquitoes. And I grew up in a rural area, so catching frogs was a rite of passage for kids. For the record, despite the common theory at the time, I never knew anyone who actually got warts from catching toads. However, my neighborhood friend Mike did once try to lick a toad after overhearing a conversation between two teenagers at the back of the school bus involving something one of their dads did while in the Navy. Nothing happened.

I can remember catching a nice frog with my brother and then bringing him back to the house to keep as a pet. One of my brothers then brought up the fact that we had Estes Rockets. If you don't remember, or maybe never heard of Estes rockets, they are little hobby rockets that come with little cardboard engines packed with a mystery propellant, quite possibly similar to the C-4 hidden in the suitcase detonated by James Bond's watch in the movie *Die Another Day*. The engines are ignited by either a car battery, a battery-powered remote device, or, in a pinch, with a wooden match lit by my toad licking friend Mike. In any case, the rocket was put on a small launchpad, and the electrodes were attached to the engine. At this point, I should say that the directions urged adult supervision when igniting rockets. This rarely happened in the 1970s. We played with Lawn Darts and with my sister Michele's Easy Bake Oven with no supervision. Some of us also went into grocery stores with handwritten notes to buy cigarettes for our mothers.

As it turned out, one of the Estes Rockets had a clear, plastic compartment located just below what would have been the payload of the vehicle, just the right size to fit, hypothetically, a small frog. Three boys, an Estes Rocket, a frog, and no adults. What could have possibly gone wrong?

We carefully placed the frog into the clear tube section of the rocket and set the rocket onto the Estes launch pad in our backyard. My oldest brother, Gary, attached the electrodes to the rocket booster engine, and we all moved back to what we considered to be a safe distance. In hindsight, it probably wasn't a safe distance as we wanted to be close enough to see the frog as the rocket took off from the pad.

This was the 1970s, so the NASA space program was in full swing. Whenever there was an Apollo rocket launch during school hours, the teachers would always wheel in a giant television with assistance from a member of the AV squad, and we would watch with great excitement and anticipation as the legendary newsman Walter Cronkite, or some other major news network anchor, would report on the countdown and launch, while the teacher was in the teacher's lounge smoking. At about the 10-second mark, the mighty Saturn V engines would fire up, and then "3, 2, 1, we have a launch!" The rockets were so huge that they appeared to be leaving Earth's gravity in slow motion, as the sounds of "oohs" and "ahhhs" would fill the classroom. The cameras would follow the rocket into the sky and to the edge of space itself, a process that lasted several minutes. It was always nothing short of spectacular.

Estes Rockets did not operate that way. There was no slow-motion effect. Basically, we would do our own NASA-style countdown, and when it got down to "liftoff" and the button was pushed, the little rocket left the launch pad at a speed of Warp factor 2. It made a loud, hissing sound as it just vanished into the sky, followed by very audible, "Wow!" and "Cool!" It actually took a few moments to find the rocket somewhere in the sky, usually as the parachute opened up. Sometimes, the chute did not open properly, and a perfectly good, brand-new Estes Rocket would smash into the ground into a hundred little pieces. Occasionally, the parachute would catch a breeze and end up wrapped around a telephone pole, or in power lines, or high up in a tree. Fortunately, none of those tragedies happened on this launch.

The rocket reached an altitude of somewhere between the height of our house and the top of the neighbor's flagpole. Or, in other words, a successful Estes Rocket launch. The parachute deployed as if on cue from NASA, and the craft landed softly in the side yard next to what would have been second base had we been playing baseball. We all ran over to the rocket, the engines still smoldering and smelling of sulfur. We all dropped to our hands and knees to get a close-up look at our amphibious rocket passenger. There was movement inside the clear plastic tube. He was alive! The frog had survived space travel with flying colors. We let him out of his spacecraft and decided he should return to his pond to live out his years, instead of living in a shoebox under my bed for quite possibly two or three days until my mother found him. And quite possibly dead as well.

Snakes, however, are a different story. I have never been much of a snake guy. Most of my friends had no problem picking up snakes and showing them to girls. As it turns out, finding random snakes, picking them up, and showing them to girls to get their attention was far more effort than was actually required. It took years to learn this fact, but a nice smile and a friendly "hello" were a far better approach. And less oogie than touching a snake. To this day, I will go out of my way to avoid any contact with snakes.

With the radio station being in a swamp, there were tons of snakes nearby. When I pulled into the parking lot at night, I would often see one or two snakes slithering off into the nearby weeds. Before I opened my car door to go to work, I would make sure that I had my hands full with my lunch, my notebook, and my giant Slurpee or Mountain Dew. When I was satisfied that I was ready, I quickly opened the door, stepped out, slammed the car door behind me, and sprinted to the front door of the radio station, giving any nearby snakes zero chance of catching me. I doubt that the kinds of snakes that lived in a swamp in Fulton, New York, were the type that chased humans, but I just don't like them.

One night, while I was on the air in the summer of 1983, one of these radio station swamp snakes got a little too close for comfort. It was around 2:30 in the morning, I had my headphones on, and I clicked the microphone on, just about to do a quick weather update on the air. As I started to speak, something caught my eye in the studio. As I turned my head, I saw a mouse scurrying along the floorboards in the studio and headed to the bathroom. I remember thinking that, after I finished my brief weather forecast (while talking up Eddy Grant's "Electric Avenue" for my radio friends), I would go catch him and toss him out of the open bathroom window. But then, the near-death part of the experience. About three seconds after the mouse ran by, a snake entered the studio and proceeded to chase the mouse into the bathroom. This was an era before automatic logging systems were installed, so there is no evidence of the on-air shriek that followed. I threw off my headphones and ran out of the studio, most likely swearing out loud. I had only seen something like that happen on television, on an episode of *Mutual of Omaha's Wild Kingdom*.

Then I remembered the now-infamous "snake memo." Every office or workplace gets dozens of memos, many sent on a daily basis. There are entire websites and social media pages dedicated to people sharing their various, and sometimes bizarre, work memos. Every now and then, one of those memos shows up that should be in the memo hall of fame if one existed. The snake memo was our hall of fame entry. Thankfully, my radio friend and one-time colleague at WKFM, Bryan Rubenau, saved a copy of the snake memo, so I will quote it directly.

"Bob is in charge while I am away. Be sure exhaust fan [sic] in transmitter room is left on. And kill any snakes that get in the building." Grammatically correct or not, a snake was in the building, and my orders were clear.

Across the hall from the WKFM studio was the studio for our AM station, WOSC, a "daytimer" signal, meaning it could only broadcast from sunrise to sunset, or whenever someone remembered to turn it on or off. In the corner of that studio, behind several enormous cobwebs and numerous dangling wires, was a special tool made for doing battle with snakes. Someone had taken a ski pole, cut the basket off the bottom, and welded a half-moon-shaped blade to the pole to create a lethal weapon meant to fight, and if need be, as per the memo, kill any snakes that get in the building. I grabbed the crude, homemade, medieval-looking weapon, turned and exited WOSC with growing confidence, and headed back into the FM studio to do battle with the serpent.

As I entered the short hallway, I looked both ways as if crossing a street, checking to make sure I was not dealing with more than one slippery intruder. In hindsight, had there been more than one snake to deal with, I would have spent the last 40-plus years in a different profession. "Electric Avenue" is a great song from 1983, but clocking in at a tight three minutes and 12 seconds in length, it was quickly nearing its final fading notes, so I knew I would have to act fast to prevent dreaded dead-air. I cautiously made my way back to the FM studio, my eyes darting around the room. There were only 20 or 30 seconds left in the song on the Technics turntable, so I bypassed the program director's actual playlist and grabbed the longest song I could find on such short notice, the Bonnie Tyler classic "Total Eclipse of the Heart," the album version at nearly seven minutes. This was normally a song reserved for bathroom breaks and pizza deliveries to the radio station, but this was potentially a life-or-death emergency. If I'd had a few more moments to choose, I would have grabbed "Freebird" or "American Pie," but desperate times call for desperate measures. (In the event of sudden gastro emergencies, DJs have a *break glass in case of emergency* container with Iron Butterfly's classic "In-A-Gadda-Da-Vida.")

The turntable revved up, and the song started just in the nick of time. With a fresh seven minutes and my trusty snake weapon, I was ready for battle. The last time I had seen the serpent, he was headed toward the open bathroom door, so I cautiously tiptoed toward the commode. It was not a large bathroom, and the studio was small, so it didn't take long for the initial search. The good news was that there was no mouse or no snake. The bad news was …there was no mouse or no snake. Even if the snake caught the mouse and ate it, I was still missing one snake, now with a full belly.

I quickly turned my attention to the studio, looking around the corners and floorboards of the room for any sudden or unusual movements. Again, nothing. Bonnie Tyler was of no help as she belted out her hit song through our studio speakers. I started to think of various horror movies and National Geographic TV specials showing huge snakes falling from ceilings and living in toilets.

The way our studio was set up, the single 45s were in a box on top of a little table next to the jock's chair to make it easy to thumb pass the songs the program director wanted me to play, to quickly find the ones I wanted to play. They were often different selections. On the floor and along the wall were larger boxes for the full-sized albums. I feared the snake had made its way into one of these boxes. I poked around these boxes with the business end of my weapon, slowly moving the albums and looking for the intruder.

After again finding nothing, I turned my attention to the radio console, which from here on will be referred to as the board, even though the console sounds more professional. The board has all the knobs, meters, microphones, doughnut crumbs, unidentified sticky stuff, and several buttons that are off-limits to everyone except the chief engineer.

Radio engineers are a different breed of cat. They survive on cold pizza, obscenities, and very little sleep. I have always felt bad having to call a broadcast engineer, regardless of the time of day, because there is a very good chance that, no matter what time it is, they might be enjoying their only downtime of the entire day. They climb radio towers in the morning, drive to remote transmitter locations throughout the day, do routine maintenance in the middle of the night, and repair upper management's kids' PlayStations when they're "not busy." I have always been careful not to touch buttons I'm not supposed to touch.

I looked behind the board at the countless wires hanging out, some connected to things, others just hanging there like cooked spaghetti that hangs out of the bottom of the colander. As I moved toward the left-hand side of the board, something very unexpected happened. The doorbell rang.

It was almost 2:30 in the morning, and someone was at the front door. There was no actual doorbell because you wouldn't want that sound of the bell to be audible over the airwaves in case the microphone was on. At our radio station, the doorbell was connected to a special light, bright enough to grab anyone's attention, even, and this is just my opinion, Stevie Wonder. Our light was bright like a controlled nuclear event. The bottom line was that someone was at the door while I was desperately trying to find a snake that was loose somewhere in the studio.

The front door was solid with no windows, so there was no way of knowing who was out there. Today, of course, you would just check out the image on a video doorbell camera to see who was out there, but this was 1983. Hot Pockets and Cabbage Patch Kids were invented that year, but nothing that would help identify strangers at the front door. With no windows to look out of or security monitors to check, I relied on the only technology available to me at the time. I turned my head sideways and put my ear to the door. I heard multiple, somewhat festive-sounding voices on the other side, and deciding there was minimal threat, I opened the door. To my surprise, the mystery guests were one of my station managers and two women. All three of them kept talking and giggling, and as I let them into the building, the boss handed me a 6-pack of cold Miller beer.

"We're going to the studio to play some tunes," he said as he walked past me into the station. "Go hang out in the production room and have a few beers for an hour or so."

Well, alright then. My boss was giving me a one-hour break at

2:30 in the morning, beer included, while he went into the radio studio with two women he had met at a bar to play their favorite songs. While I'm sure this is not what Marconi had in mind when he invented radio, at that moment, I knew I had the best job in the world. I had just popped open a nice cold Miller and taken a sip when reality slapped me in the face like one of the Three Stooges. The late-night guests were in the main radio studio, and so was a wild snake. I am not a snake expert, so I couldn't identify its specific variety, only that more than likely, it was not venomous. However, I would have still described it as deadly because if it surprised me there in the middle of the night, I would have had a heart attack.

I grabbed my homemade snake weapon and headed out of the production room down the short hall to the window that looked into the studio. While I didn't want to appear like some kind of weirdo watching them through the glass, I did want to somehow alert my colleague of the unwelcome guest that may show up and ruin any chance he had with either one, or both, of his guests. I seriously doubted there was any chance that all three of them would end up going anywhere together, but there he was partying with two women in the studio. He was jamming David Bowie's "Let's Dance" at high volume, and his two friends were indeed dancing. They didn't see me, so I stood there and stared like the Rain Man watching *Jeopardy*.

As the party on the other side of the glass continued, I looked around the studio through the window for any sign of the snake. Both women were now dancing barefoot, holding their shoes in one hand and a beer in the other. The GM had my headphones on and was cueing up the next song. As far as I remember, he never turned the microphone on and never said anything on the air during that hour. He was just DJing a private party in the studio, with the tunes being broadcast over the airwaves. I must admit, he was having the time of his life. As I stood there looking through the glass window at the impromptu party at 3:00 in the morning, with a Miller beer in one hand and a snake-killing ski pole in the other, I remember thinking this would not be happening had I been a chemical engineer. I loved it!

As the time wore on and the music continued, I became more confident that the snake had either escaped through a hole in the wall or was all coiled up inside studio equipment and not interested in showing himself. Not being a snake expert, I didn't even know if it was a male or female snake. I'm pretty sure I don't know how to tell the difference. I left the main studio window and went back to my beer in the production room as the dance party continued. The music was loud enough that I could make out the tunes through the supposed soundproof walls. I heard "Maniac" from the Flashdance soundtrack, Lionel Richie's "All Night Long," "Come Dancing," by the Kinks, "Beat It" from Michael Jackson, and "Karma Chameleon," from the Culture Club." The summer of 1983 had some great tunes.

At about 3:30, the volume of the studio monitors decreased to a level at which I could no longer make out the songs. After a few more minutes of relative quiet, the studio door opened, and out walked the boss and his female guests, high heels still in hand. The women walked past me and to the front door, offering me little more than a toothy grin as they headed out to the parking lot. The upper manager briefly stopped and extended his hand for a handshake, saying only, "Hope the beer was cold enough." I nodded in the affirmative as he joined his guests outside, closing the door behind him. I locked the door and made my way back into the main studio.

As I took my seat behind the console, I couldn't help but notice the strong aroma of perfume and cigarette smoke, combined with Old Spice, beer, and pleather. My boss had definitely been here. I also looked around for any sign of the snake but found nothing. Good. As I checked the equipment and grabbed my headphones, I noticed the request line ringing. I pushed the button to answer the line with the standard, "Magic 104.7." The caller was excited.

"Hey man, lovin' the tunes you've been playing for the past hour, and no talkin.' You should do that all the time." I gave him a half-hearted, "Thanks, man," as I hung up the phone.

So much for the well-researched playlist and banter. I decided to finish the rest of the beer and tell no one of this night. Until now, of course.

CHAPTER 5

NOVEMBER RAIN AND TATYANA

I have met so many incredible people and made some lifelong friends during my 40-plus years in broadcasting. One of my best friends from radio was the late Dave White. Dave was an unbelievable news anchor for WSYR when I worked with him in the mid-1980s. The 570 WSYR newsroom was second to none, world-class top to bottom. I would have put that newsroom and on-air staff up against any other news radio staff in the country at that time, and Dave was a big part of that success.

Dave was a fun guy, a great conversationalist, and he looked a little bit like Mark Twain. We also shared a love of the outdoors. With Dave and a few of his friends, we would go camping every summer, and by camping, I mean we'd go into the woods, set up a tent, and then go to a bar. Okay, we weren't exactly trailblazers. Roughing it with these guys meant there was a line at the diner for breakfast. There are plenty of camping stories to share, mostly involving beer, and a Polish vodka called Wisniowka, which I had no idea how to spell until 10 seconds ago when I googled it. Wisniowka is a strong vodka that tastes like a combination of kerosene and bad decisions. It may very well fuel rockets on future NASA missions to

Mars. I was introduced to this bottle of mayhem by my Adirondack Mountain friend, Richard. Any book about him will require proof of age and will only be available on the dark web.

As it turns out, my camping friends were also my hockey game friends. Every year or so, we plan a trip to a different city in Canada to watch an NHL game, and by that, I mean we go to strip clubs.

Here's a tip for the ladies, and I know I am violating a big bro-code here. But if your husband or boyfriend says he is going to Canada for any reason…hockey weekend, maple syrup convention, a Bryan Adams concert, or to watch the changing of the guards at the Parliament building in Ottawa, the chance that he is also going to a strip club is approximately 100 percent, plus or minus about 0 percent.

It's really quite simple: we go to strip clubs, we give our hard-earned money to dancers, and they dance. That's it. Invariably, there will be a guy who is absolutely convinced that a particular dancer, usually named Cheyenne, or Angel, or Natasha, truly likes him. He is totally convinced that under a different set of circumstances, namely that he is not currently married, has no children, has an actual job, and is not stinking drunk, that this particular young lady would ride off on the back of a Harley with him like a girl in a Bob Seger song. To my knowledge, this has never actually happened, but the fantasy plays out at gentlemen's clubs around the world every night of the week.

Ottawa is a frequent destination for my hockey buddies and me. From my house in Cicero, New York, we can drive right to the Canadian capital city in less than three and a half hours, unless we stop at the duty-free store at the border to buy cigars and liquor. Or stop at Canadian Tire just because it is an awesome store. Or make a stop at a pharmacy to purchase Canadian Tylenol pills, more commonly known as "222s." These are common painkillers here in the States, but in Canada, they add codeine and can be purchased over-the-counter for about eight dollars for a huge bottle. In the USA, they require a prescription and cost about the same as good tickets to a Taylor Swift concert. Anyway, these stops along the way can add a good 45 minutes or more to the road trip.

This particular road trip to Ottawa featured a Friday night Senators game. (Pro-tip...don't mention to the wife or significant other that the weekend hockey game is actually on Friday, so technically, the trip could be an overnight excursion instead of a two-night party. You're welcome.) The beauty of the Friday night game is that it frees up the entire day and night on Saturday, meaning it is then possible to either visit some of the amazing museums Ottawa has to offer, or to locate and visit most, if not all, of the strip clubs in the city. For the record, when we put it to a vote among the four of us, museums actually received one vote. True democracy in action. Science also tells us that "for every action, there is an equal and opposite reaction." Long story short, that one friend has never been invited to join us again in Canada.

Nothing beats watching professional hockey in person at a great arena. Another pro tip...when planning a visit to Ottawa to watch a Senators game, make sure your hotel room isn't actually in Ottawa. The arena is in Kanata, Ontario, a fine suburb of Ottawa and a healthy 30 or so minute bus ride from downtown, and if you have a few pre-game beers, the restroomless bus ride will seem endless. Depending on which side of Ottawa your hotel room is, it may actually be more convenient to go to Montreal to see a Canadiens game. The Senators played the Buffalo Sabres that Friday night, which filled the many great bars and restaurants in downtown Ottawa and the popular Byward Market.

The excellent scheduling of the Friday night game left Saturday wide open to discover the amazing culture of Canada's beautiful capital city, and by that I mean the Canadian ballet, Canadian folk dancing, or whatever you want to call strip clubs. After walking around Ottawa for a while and conducting extensive research, which meant one of the guys pointed and said, "Look, there's one," we settled on a gentlemen's club about four blocks from our hotel.

Again, having gone to the Senator's game the night before, we had the entire day to ourselves. It was not even 4:00 in the after-noon when we entered the club, which, as far as I'm concerned, is the best time to visit a gentlemen's club. The big crowds and bach-elor parties don't show up until later in the evening, so the dancers have more time to actually pay attention to you. In fact, on that particular Saturday afternoon, the crowd consisted of our group of four and one guy sitting alone in front of the stage. Every exotic dance club in the world has a guy like this. All alone in front of the stage. (It should be noted here that, as much as I enjoy a good gentlemen's club as much as the next guy, I never want to be THAT guy.) The afternoon dancers were finishing up, and some of the nighttime dancers were arriving. They must have been preparing for a huge nighttime crowd, as the customers were outnumbered a good 10 to 1. I remember thinking, "This must be what girls feel like going to a RUSH concert."

The great aspect of going to a gentlemen's club off hours is that the dancers will often come right to your table and sit down with you. That was the case on this Saturday afternoon as no less than six lovely ladies pulled up chairs and sat with us. Don't misunder-stand, they were still working. They each made their obligatory lap dance sales pitch, but then they realized they were dealing with four middle-aged guys on a budget, so they just hung out with us, and we bought them a round of drinks. (Pro-tip...buying a round of drinks at a gentlemen's club costs roughly the same as tuition at a small private school.)

The lovely young lady who sat down next to me was a pretty Russian girl named Tatyana from Moscow, which meant her real name was probably Becky, and she was most likely from Kingston, Ontario. The unexpected icebreaker was Syracuse University sports. As it turned out, Tatyana was a huge SU basketball fan. SU basketball was apparently often aired on a Canadian sports TV channel. Coincidentally, the radio station where I have worked for most of my career is also the flagship station for Syracuse basket-ball, and at the time, I hosted a weekly hour-long call-in show with

Hall of Fame head coach Jim Boeheim. Bingo. I was instantly a rock star. Suddenly, her fake Russian accent gave way to her native, and far more attractive, Canadian accent.

"What's Fab Melo like, eh?" she asked, referring to a player on the team.

After another beer (costing the equivalent of a quarter tank of gas) and some chit chat about SU players Dion Waiters and CJ Fair, my booze confidence grew. In real, non-beer life, I am somewhat shy and actually a bit socially awkward, somewhere between Toby from *The Office* and Milhouse on *The Simpsons*. For the record, when I was younger, I was never able to talk to girls. My "hall pass" woman is Shania Twain, and in the radio business, there is a very small chance that I could actually meet her someday, perhaps introducing her at a concert. My wife has always given me permission to flirt with Shania if that opportunity ever presented itself. She didn't actually say it that way. I believe her direct quote was, "Oh yes, please do! I gotta see this."

But after three or four overpriced bottles of ice-cold Labatt Blue at a Canadian strip club, I became Ryan Gosling, minus the looks, abs, and sophistication. Suddenly, I knew exactly what to say. I grabbed my bottle of Labatt, took a slow swig of beer, all the while looking directly at Tatyana, and put the bottle down on the uneven table.

"So, why don't you show me the rest of that lightning bolt tattoo?" I said, staring right at her. My friends were shocked at my newfound swagger that accompanied that line. I even surprised myself. Tatyana smiled, looked down at the tattoo that started just below her right shoulder, traveled all the way down her right side, and disappeared into her skintight red spandex pants, which were dotted with random rips and holes that added to the fantasy of her outfit.

She then looked me directly in the eye and said — and this is a direct quote that has affected my level of confidence ever since —"That's not a lightning bolt, it's barbed wire." It should be noted that this is around the time in my life when I began to wear glasses, which I was not wearing at the time.

The brief moment of swagger was gone, but business is business. Tatyana stood up from the table, took me by the hand, and led me to the VIP lounge, which was basically a few small couches on the other side of a short partition wall that vaguely separated the VIP area from the main floor. It reminded me of the old restaurants back in the day that had smoking and non-smoking sections separated by absolutely nothing. In essence, you could enjoy some other guy's VIP experience just by glancing over to the other side of the room.

The very pretty and petite brunette Tatyana led me over to one of the small couches behind a tiny circular table and sat down next to me with her drink, and we chatted. The dancer on the main floor was finishing up her set, gyrating to the Def Leppard classic "Pour Some Sugar on Me," a great rock song played at every gentlemen's club around the world probably 15 times per night, per club. That song is to exotic dancers what "On The Road Again" is to truckers. The extra chat time with a dancer in the VIP lounge while another song winds down is free of charge, one of the unwritten rules of exotic dance clubs.

The small afternoon crowd applauded "Omega" as she left the dimly lit stage. The house DJ excitedly instructed all six or seven of us in attendance to "put your hands together for your next dancer," and I am not making this up, "Jenna Bush." I doubt that was her real first name, but after watching her performance, it may well have been her real last name.

Tatyana stood up, shook her long black hair back and forth, and straddled my knees as the next song began. The DJ hit the play button, and the opening notes of "November Rain" from Guns N' Roses filled the room. November freaking Rain, nearly nine minutes of a classic rock ballad! This was going to be my VIP private dance song. Nine minutes of the lovely Tatyana and her amazing lightning bolt/barbed wire tattoo that started under her shoulder and disappeared into her red spandex pants. I had hit the jackpot, the Holy Grail of a gentlemen's club dance. A nine-minute VIP lounge dance song was the equivalent of watching a hockey brawl, and the goalies meet at center ice and drop their gloves. It just doesn't happen that often.

Tatyana stared into my eyes as Axl Rose started in with the lyrics, which ironically begin with a line about looking into your eyes. She slid her hands up to her petite shoulders, never leaving her deep gaze into my beer-infused eyes. This was about to be epic. A smoking hot little fake Russian exotic dancer was sitting in my lap, staring into my eyes and about to remove her top with a nine-minute rock classic blaring through the speakers, when something happened that had never happened to me in a strip club before that moment. Ever. Her cell phone rang. (For the record, her ringtone was the Michigan University fight song.)

She instantly put the straps back up onto her shoulders, dropped the fake Russian accent, and said in perfectly easy-to-understand Canadian English, "I am so sorry, but I have to take this call."

She then produced a tiny little purse seemingly out of thin air that, until that moment, I had not seen at all. It was like an awesome magic trick that would have easily fooled Penn and Teller. She opened it up, removed and put on a pair of really thick reading glasses, and then took out her little flip phone and answered it. My nine-minute Guns N' Roses dream lap dance had taken a turn. Axl and Slash were a good two minutes into November Rain as I sat on the VIP couch watching a beautiful Russian exotic dancer with an awesome full-body lightning bolt/barbed wire tattoo, wearing Coke-bottle-thick reading glasses, listening intently and nodding while on her flip phone. It was not exactly a Hallmark Channel holiday movie moment.

After a few minutes of listening, she said, "I understand," to the person on the other end of the phone call. She closed the flip phone, took a deep breath, and turned to me with the news.

"I am so sorry about that. My boyfriend got arrested today."

I briefly stared and nodded at Tatyana, trying to convey my concern for her unfortunate and stressful situation, but simultaneously wanted to ask her, "What does this have to do with 'November Rain,' and seeing the rest of your tattoo?" But that's not what came out.

"That's awful," I said. But then, my big mistake. And I knew I had erred the moment the words left my mouth. I added, "So, what happened?"

The beautiful, petite fake Russian dancer with the thick Coke-bottle glasses sat side-saddle on my lap and burst into tears.

"He's wanted in New Mexico for stealing heavy machinery." I blinked several times, trying to absorb that sentence, one I had never heard uttered before. The tears were falling by the bucket-ful, and in typical male fashion, I had no idea what to say. Some men have a better working knowledge of how to calm down a sobbing exotic dancer. I am not one of them. I was just patting her on her upper back, trying to reassure her by saying what most every guy would probably say at a time like that.

"Oh, it's ok. Everything will work out. Just wait, you'll be fine." I was also thinking, "Do I still owe her $20 for this?" The more she sobbed, the more I patted.

"There, there now, things always seem worse than they really are." I tried my best to sound like a dad. Stuttering through tears and sniffles, she looked at me. Her eyes looked enormous through those thick glasses. She stammered in broken syllables.

"You don't understand, now I don't have anyone to watch my kids." While I genuinely felt bad for her and her situation, this had quickly become the worst fantasy ever. She put her pretty little fake Russian head on my shoulder and continued to cry. November Rain was nearly over. I also wanted to cry. But I continued to try and reassure her that things would work out.

"There must be someone who can give you a hand," I said. "What about your parents? Are they nearby?"

She stopped crying for a moment and leaned back away from

me, looked me right in the eyes, took another deep breath, and said in flawless Canadian dialect a sentence I will remember for the rest of my life.

"My parents live in Vancouver, and they think I'm a personal trainer." This was just not going well.

"November Rain" was coming to an end. What had begun as the ultimate gentlemen's club fantasy with a beautiful Russian exotic dancer and an epic nine-minute classic rock ballad had ended with a mostly clothed Canadian girl weeping on my lap. The song and fantasy were both over, my beer was empty, and I would be asked to leave in a few moments. It was like I was single again.

The DJ screamed into the microphone, "Alright, guys, keep it going for Omega as we bring her back to the stage for her nightly shower dance!" The small crowd applauded as he started the next song, "Magic Power" by the band Triumph. There is a rule in Canada that a certain percentage of music programming must include Canadian artists, so Triumph fit the bill.

Tatyana stood up, wiped the tears away, removed her thick reading glasses, and started to dance again for me. She was an absolute trooper. She was fully prepared to perform a "do-over" for me and dance to Magic Power. Although I really did appreciate the effort, I politely held up my hand.

"Oh gosh, I'm all set, but thank you," I implored. As I stood up, I handed her two $20 bills. "Maybe you can put that towards a babysitter for a night," I added. (For the record, I have no idea how much babysitters are paid in Canada.) She stood up, got up on her toes, and gave me a little kiss on the cheek. I smiled.

If this had been a Hallmark movie, I would have quit my job and moved to Vermont to open a coffee shop with Tatyana. But this was Canada, I'd had a few beers, and I had just given 40 dollars to a stripper so she could get a babysitter. I still wonder how much of that story she told me was actually true. Don't tell my friends.

CHAPTER 6

THE COAL MINER'S DAUGHTER

It had been a long day of golf at the beautiful Shenandoah golf course at the Turning Stone Resort and Casino in Verona, about halfway down the New York State Thruway between Syracuse and Utica. One of the benefits of being a local radio host who likes to golf is that you get invited to play in many charity golf tournaments. It is impossible to make a long day of golf sound anything but fun, especially at a facility like the Turning Stone. On this particular day in June of 2014, I had the privilege of playing in an event called the Towsley Pro-Am Golf Tournament, a benefit for the Upstate Medical University Foundation, with my morning radio show partner, and single-digit handicap golfer, Dave Coombs. We had played in several of these types of events over the years. We had even won a couple of them. We could pass off playing in these tournaments to our program manager back at the station as a chance to schmooze with clients, which we did, but mainly, they were just a lot of fun.

Among the items in the golf tournament goodie bag was a voucher for some free play at the casino, a fun way to take the sting out of my mediocre round of golf. So, after a post-tournament meal at the clubhouse, I headed over to the gaming floor to try my luck. And by that, I mean hand my money over to a slot machine. I went to look for the only slot machine I liked at the time, *Ghostbusters,* based on the comedy film. I found the game, but a young woman was playing it, so I grabbed a beer and stood back to wait my turn.

I sipped my long-neck beer and glanced around the busy gaming floor, and like every casino I've ever been to, it sounded like everyone was winning, except me. Lights were flashing, bells were ringing, and every so often, the scream of some lucky player at the roulette wheel. I am not much of a gambler, although I enjoy the excitement and energy of a casino. The only time I have ever had any kind of luck gambling was on one of those 24-hour "down and back" bus trips from Syracuse to Atlantic City in the 1980s. A buddy of mine worked at our local power company and roped me into the bus trip with many of his coworkers. My friend drove a hard bargain.

"I looked at the list of people going, it's like 35 women, plus you and me," he said. "It's a whole bus full of girls! Do you want to g...?" I blurted out "hell yeah" before he finished saying the word "go."

We met the bus at 6:00 on that fall Saturday morning, giddy with excitement for the 6-hour trip to Atlantic City with 35 girls. I hopped on the bus with my buddy Tom right behind me, took two steps, then stopped. I paused for a moment and looked around.

"Are we on the right bus?" I asked my friend Tom.

"Yes," he said. "There is only one bus and we're on it."

I turned back around and slowly made my way toward the back of the bus, walking past all of the girls on the bus. Tom and I were in our mid-20s, and from what I could see, we were the youngest people on the bus by a solid 40 years. The six-hour trip to Atlantic City would be Tom, me, and 35 women between the ages of the Golden Girls and Mamie Eisenhower.

After taking our seats, I turned to Tom and asked, "Didn't you check the list ahead of time? How many girls our age do you know who have the first names of Doris, Harriet, or Maude?!"

"I guess I never thought of it," Tom admitted. "I just saw a bunch of women's names. At the least, the ride should be quiet." Ever the optimist. For the record, many of the senior ladies started drinking before the bus made it to Binghamton, about an hour into the trip.

Overall, the trip was fun. The bus arrived at the Tropicana, and within 20 minutes, I had won $120 playing blackjack. We then went up and down the famed Atlantic City boardwalk, stopping into the many different casinos, playing various slot machines, occasional hands of blackjack, spins of the roulette wheel, and lots of video poker. As they said in *The Hangover,* I was on a heater. I won some money at every casino we visited, and at every type of game. A $100 here, $120 there, another $75 somewhere else. I was even dealt a royal flush on a video poker game that paid out $250, all in quarters. This was the 1980s, long before winners' payouts came out of machines in the form of receipts that had to be brought to a cashier's window or cash machine for payout. During that time period, you would walk up and down the boardwalk with buckets of quarters from the various casinos. When you won a jackpot, the sound of quarters pouring out of a slot machine was one of the all-time great experiences. While I'm sure the newer, updated machines are more efficient, and by that I mean more profitable, I surely miss those old slot machines.

After all was said and done, I had won $1,200! I was returning with a wallet full of cash. It was by far the most I had ever won at anything. I decided to use my gambling winnings to treat myself to something I had never had before, a really nice 10-speed bicycle. She was a beauty, a gorgeous navy blue frame with slick ram's horn handlebars. At the time, I lived on the near westside of Syracuse, and I instantly loved riding through the hilly neighborhoods of Tipperary Hill and Strathmore. I figured that bike would give me several years of exercise, fresh air, and long bike trips with my friends.

The following Saturday, after my successful trip to Atlantic City, someone stole my beautiful bicycle right out of our garage in the middle of the day while I was mowing the backyard. Several years later, I found out who had stolen my beautiful 10-speed bike. The guy then sold it, using the proceeds to help fund gender-affirming surgery. In essence, I was a trailblazer. I hope she was happy with the results. Hell, I might be friends with her on Facebook and don't even know it. Gambling money. Easy come, easy go.

At the Turning Stone on this particular evening, the casino was busy. It seems most casinos are busy these days, day and night. As I stood waiting my turn at the *Ghostbusters* slot machine, I suddenly became aware of familiar music. I turned and walked toward the resort's showroom and recognized the voice and songs of Loretta Lynn. The legendary country music singer was performing in the showroom, and I listened while standing in the wide corridor that separates the casino from the showroom for quite a while. I knew all of the songs.

My parents were both fans of country music, and Loretta Lynn. I suspect many in my age group could say the same about their parents. The down-home tunes resonated with my mother, who grew up on a farm in the Adirondack Mountains of northern New York. And my father knew the music as well, probably learning the songs after befriending many southern boys while in the army in Korea and picking up on their taste in music.

When I was young, my parents' bedroom was across the hall from the bedroom I shared with my younger brother Michael. At night, with the bedroom doors closed, my parents would stack six or seven country western record albums on their Hi-Fi stereo and listen to them as they fell asleep. If you are of a certain age, you would remember that as one album finished, the needle would pick up, the arm would move away, and the next album would magically fall onto the turntable. The needle would set back down on the next album and play that one in its entirety. Hours and hours of the Columbia House collection of country western classics, from

Johnny Cash, to Patsy Cline, Glen Campbell, Hank Williams, and every hit from Loretta Lynn.

I sat down on a bench near the closed doors of the showroom of the Turning Stone, smiling while listening to "Coal Miner's Daughter," "Don't Come Home A-Drinkin' (With Lovin' On Your Mind)," "I'm A Honky Tonk Girl," and all the hits from the first lady of country music. I don't own any country music albums, but I know this music. I sat and listened to Loretta Lynn for a good 40 minutes or so and enjoyed every moment.

At one point, the showroom door opened, and a couple left the concert, disappearing into the casino. A friend of mine who worked at the showroom emerged from the open door and saw me, and asked if I wanted to sneak in and catch a few tunes. I appreciated the offer, but chose to sit on the bench and listen to the music muffled through the closed doors, imagining I was 10 years old again, with my parents young, healthy, and alive on the other side of the doors, also enjoying the music of Loretta Lynn. It made me smile.

CHAPTER 7

PEPPERMINT PETE

As I have previously mentioned, I decided to leave my first radio job at the station in Herkimer after much debate and serious thought, but mainly because my $25.00 Christmas bonus check from the company bounced. This is not an uncommon story from radio people. Often, radio stations are owned and operated by guys with no real broadcast experience. I'm convinced that there are guys who own radio stations because they won the deed and license to the station in a game of craps. That method of ownership may not be as common today, as there are huge corporations that routinely buy large groups of radio stations, who then promptly invite current longtime employees to sign up for their generous severance packages. Every radio broadcaster has at least one story about working for an owner who would cut costs in unique ways.

For example, the studios for the station where the program director left us the "kill any snakes" memo also had a handwritten note taped to the wall suggesting that the air staff "wear hats and gloves while in the studio during winter months," further evidence of the cost-saving idea to have no heating system in the building. The Herkimer experience should have been enough to point me in a different career direction, but just like Michael Corleone suggested in *The Godfather,* they always find a way to pull you back in.

I thought I had a pretty decent plan. My idea was to get my old summer job back at Syracuse University, where I could work full-time, get some great benefits, and more importantly, take six credits of college courses every semester and eventually earn a bachelor's degree from the famed Newhouse School of Communications, all free of charge. I was all set to put my plan into motion when my buddy Tim called and, to continue the theme, made me an offer I couldn't refuse.

"They have an opening over here at Channel 3 to operate the teleprompter during newscasts." Tim was a studio tech at the local NBC affiliate in Syracuse, WSTM-TV3. I asked what anyone would ask, even though I was pretty sure I already knew the answer.

"How much does it pay?" Shrewd.

"Well," Tim explained, "It's basically minimum wage, and it's only about 21 hours per week, but I might be able to get you a spot on Saturday Showboat. That would give you an extra 4 hours a week."

"Hmm," I thought. I could either work at a major university and earn a free college degree, or go run the teleprompter, and get an extra 4 hours of minimum wage pay per week working on a local Saturday morning kids' TV show. Quickly doing the math in my head, I answered.

"I'm in. Sounds fun!"

Another solid yes response to a question. This is why many radio and television people still have housemates well into their 40s.

I enjoyed working in the television studio, running the tele-prompter for the local newscasts. The prompter operator wields more power in a news studio than you'd think, having the ability to dictate the pace at which news anchors read the news script. I was amazed at how much responsibility was given to a minimum wage employee, almost as amazed at how much fun I could have scrolling non-news, and often adult-oriented, material across the prompter in an attempt to bring an unscripted smile to a weekend on-air talent. It was good fun.

I also occasionally ran a studio camera for the weekly bowling show that was recorded on Thursday evenings for playback the following Sunday morning. The show was called "Syracuse Bowls," and when I worked on that show, I ran the camera that was pointed at the scoreboard. It was without a doubt the easiest camera shot at the TV station, and after setting the camera shot before the show began, I would get the following instructions from the director through my headset.

"Good, now don't touch it."

It was impossible to screw up. Every now and then, I was called upon to add the score to the bowling scoreboard by taking a Sharpie pen and, with the camera on, put an "X" for a strike, or the diagonal line for a spare, or quickly do the math and add the correct score. For the record, I never totaled the score incorrectly. My three semesters of engineering classes at SUNY Buffalo were finally paying dividends. So, for those who watched Syracuse Bowls in the early 1980s, that was my right hand that was occasionally shown on television. I was officially in show business.

A few weeks after starting the job at Channel 3, my buddy Tim announced that he would be leaving his position at the TV station. Tim also worked in the studio. His other duties included checking the daily studio logs to make sure all of the commercials were in place for the next day's broadcasts. That is a task that is now computerized, but back in the day, it was done manually, like changing gears in a car or flipping albums on a turntable. It might be slightly more efficient, but it's not nearly as interesting or fun. But here's where my extra hours came into play.

Tim was also a personality on the long-running local Saturday morning kids show, "Saturday Showboat," portraying the character "Bobo the Hobo." Again, this was 1982, when the term hobo was not meant as anything derogatory, and if anything, it was something several of my friends and I aspired to. I have long fantasized about hopping a train car with nothing but a bindle of clothes just to see where I ended up. Not knowing the train's final destination would have been the excitement of the journey. If it were possible to earn a living as a hobo, I would have done it. Then again, earning anything as a hobo would have defeated the entire purpose of being a hobo and ruined its attraction.

Tim spoke with the producers of the kids' show and convinced them that I would be a suitable replacement for his character. Bobo's "Saturday Showboat" farewell was my first appearance on the show. Although the program aired every Saturday morning at 7:00, it was actually "recorded live" on Monday evenings at 7:00. Before that first appearance, I had to come up with a costume and a character, as I could never replace Bobo "the Hobo." Tim was well over 6 feet tall and skinny. I was 5 feet 8, and somewhat round. When we stood right next to each other, we looked like the number 10. The kids would have immediately noticed.

Before that first show, I went to the expansive Channel 3 studio storage area to look for some kind of prop or outfit. I wish everyone from Central New York could have taken a tour of that backstage area, as it was filled with all of the cool props and sets from a youth spent watching local Saturday morning and afternoon television. Most impressive was the model used for the opening of the legendary local show *Monster Movie Matinee,* a horror movie program that featured the characters Dr. E. Nick Witty and Epal. On television, the haunted house was a huge old mansion enveloped by a sinister and mysterious fog. The actual model used for the opening sequence was no bigger than a good-sized birdhouse with a spot to put dry ice to create the fog. The magic of television.

There were also props and set pieces from the equally legendary local TV show *Salty Sam's Super Saturday.* Pulling the curtain back here, the guy portraying Salty Sam was the same guy who was Epal from *Monster Movie Matinee,* Bill Everett. I had the pleasure of working with Bill at WSYR radio in the early 1980s when he was the production director. I remember the first time I met Bill and thinking, "Oh my God, that's Salty Sam!" I went into his studio to say hi and introduce myself, and the first thing he said to me stopped me in my tracks.

"You'll have to excuse me, I have no stomach." That was followed by a hearty laugh. To this day, I have no idea what that meant. He also told me that he was Epal from *Monster Movie Matinee*, a tidbit I hadn't known prior to that moment.

"Where did the name Epal come from?" I asked. He dropped some more knowledge on me.

"My real last name is Lape," he continued. "Epal is just Lape spelled backwards." If that were in text form, I would have responded with some kind of "mind blown" emoji.

After rummaging through the back rooms of the studio, I ran across an old red and white striped blazer once worn by yet another local television legend, Denny Sullivan. I then found an old styrofoam skimmer hat and a colorful, oversized bowtie. Voila! Instant kids' TV show outfit.

The format for the production of *Saturday Showboat* was very loose, with just an outline of the hour, with what each character would be doing and how long the segment would be. When the taping of that first show began, my character still did not have an official name yet, so we put it to the young viewers to help come up with a good name. Dozens of suggestions came in from all over Central New York and Northern Pennsylvania, as an affiliate there also carried the weekly show.

As we were sifting through the creative suggestions that arrived in the mail, one of the guys from the sports department wandered by and asked what we were doing.

"Glenn started on *Saturday Showboat* this week, and we're looking for a good name for his character," the show's production director replied. I showed him the red and white striped blazer I would be wearing, and he blurted out the first thing that came to him.

"How about Peppermint Pete?"

It was perfect! Peppermint Pete sounded fun, and who doesn't like peppermint? The suggestion was an instant hit. I assumed that Peppermint Pete may have been a nickname or child's toy the sports guy remembered from his youth, so I asked.

"Where did you come up with that?"

"It's something you can request from escorts in Las Vegas. Don't ask."

I didn't, but as it turns out, apparently, a Peppermint Pete is something you would pay extra for on the Strip in Sin City. For good reason, we never shared this information with the audience. I loved the name, and the kids loved the name. As far as we were concerned, my new Saturday morning kids' TV show character was named for a tasty, minty, holiday treat, and that's all they needed to know.

As Peppermint Pete, in the following weeks and months, I would play banjo, teach kids how to juggle, and interact with the other characters on *Saturday Showboat,* including Uncle Don, George the Magician, and The Crafty Lady. And because the show aired at 7:00 on Saturday mornings, and I was 22 years old and living at home, I really only saw the show once, and that was because I was just coming home from a long Friday night of partying. Banjo-playing, kids' show character by day, beer-sipping partier by night. The best part was that, although the show was "recorded live" in real time and therefore took one hour to do, I was paid for 4 hours of work. Given my salary of a little over minimum wage multiplied by my total hours worked, I was effectively paid a grand total of about 13 dollars and 40 cents a week to be Peppermint Pete. Ah, local TV in the early 1980s.

CHAPTER 8

SEEING A LEGEND
IN THE DESERT

"Mark said he can go, you gotta come with us to Nipton."
That's all it took. That's usually all it takes to embark on
a road trip with my good friend Tom Langmyer. Everybody has,
or should have, a friend like Tom. Always ready for a road trip, an
adventure, a long drive, a greasy burger, and a beer. Anything that
produces one of those lifetime memories. Tom is a good guy and
a great friend. We worked together at WSYR-AM and WYYY-FM in
Syracuse in the mid-1980s and early 1990s. They were two powerhouse radio stations, both highly regarded nationally in that era,
and Tom was a big reason for that recognition.

"So exactly where are we going this time?"I asked.

"The world's largest working thermometer. It's in the Mojave
Desert near a restaurant called Bun Boy in Baker, California," he
replied over the phone. He added the three words that have always
hooked me into a road trip. "We gotta' go."

Tom had a distinct advantage when taking these trips west. He
was the general manager of the legendary Midwest radio station
WGN, and as a result, had easy access to dozens of daily, direct
non-stop flights to McCarran International Airport in Las Vegas

from his home in Chicago. I still lived near Syracuse, New York, where we had, until fairly recently, a very limited choice of daily flights, primarily on the type of small commuter planes where the in-flight entertainment consisted of reading the ingredients on the tiny package of pretzels handed out by flight attendants. Many of those flights also required boarding from the tarmac after walking outside the terminal.

On this particular trip, we each had a goal. Tom wanted to see the world's largest thermometer, his childhood friend Mark wanted to see Death Valley, and I wanted to ride the Desperado. The Desperado is an amazing roller coaster built in the desert at a casino called Buffalo Bill's on the border of Nevada and California in Primm Valley. It's an area that I imagine is visited by people using several different aliases, either running from something or somehow just ending up there. Gamblers at these tables, far from the glitz of the Las Vegas strip, are people of the desert with smokers' coughs and sun-dried skin. Real people. I absolutely love it.

We stayed in the small desert town of Nipton, California. Nipton is an old miner's town that consists of a general store, a campground, the historic Nipton Hotel, and at least one stray cat. It's about an hour from Las Vegas, and as the saying goes, "It might not be the end of the world, but by God you can see it from there." The Nipton Hotel is really more of a bed and breakfast kind of place, with each rustic room equipped with earplugs. The fabulous old hotel is set back about 40 yards or so from the Union Pacific railway, and these trains run around the clock on a very regular schedule, day and night, hence the earplugs.

The legendary Nipton Hotel was our base camp for the weekend. Our first stop, as I suspect it is with most every road trip with friends, was the liquor store. Almost every road trip I have ever been on with friends has begun with the purchase of some kind of alcohol, usually a beer at the airport bar or the hotel lounge. I have always been amazed by travelers at airports who can belly up to an airport bar and have the "Texas-sized" beer in a giant glass mug in the shape of a cowboy boot at 8:00 or 9:00 in the morning. Regardless of age, guys on a road trip become college freshmen, and the transformation is almost instant. The liquor store in Nipton was located in the general store, and I settled on my favorite adult beverage of moderation when not having beer or wine. The Captain. As in Captain Morgan's and Diet Coke. I have no idea why the Diet Coke, I'm not fooling anybody.

Although it was getting late that Friday night in the desert, we hopped into the rental car for the half-hour drive along Route 164 to the town of Searchlight, Nevada, for some quick gambling and a bite to eat. Being a small, unincorporated town in Nevada, the options were few. We settled on a place called "Terrible's Roadhouse." If you were making a movie about a prison escapee hiding in the desert under an assumed name, this is where he might be employed. We loved it.

Terrible's Roadhouse is the restaurant inside Terrible's Casino, a gaming and dining spot favored by the locals. Before dinner, we decided to try our luck at the slot machines. None of us were particularly avid gamblers, and by that, I mean we usually lost. However, after 30 minutes or so of pulling arms on slot machines and sipping beers, we all met near the restaurant to compare notes and tally our winnings. As it turned out, the three of us managed to win a total of almost 90 dollars! We sat down at a table near a large window, looked at the old menus, and figured out we had won enough for the three of us to enjoy a steak dinner. Just a few hours into our trip, and we were already, to quote Charlie Sheen, "Winning!"

An hour or so after eating a pretty good steak and finishing our beers, we headed back down Route 164, also known as the old Nipton Road, back to the fabulous Nipton Hotel for a night of being awakened hourly by the passing of a huge train. That is a big part of the charm of the hotel. It was exciting lying in bed, just about ready to doze off, when suddenly hearing the far-off whistle of yet another enormous Union Pacific train making its way from

Long Beach, California, to parts east, passing within 100 feet or so of the Nipton Hotel. Although each room came with the earplugs, we chose to go without for fear of missing one of the trains. It was pretty awesome.

Don't get me wrong, sleep rocks. I love sleep. In recent years, I've come to love going to bed on a Friday night by 8:30, or about the time I used to go out and meet up with friends to start the weekend. The first thing I think about after getting out of bed in the morning is going back to bed later that evening. Nothing beats a good night's sleep. But occasionally, there are moments or events that make interrupted sleep worthwhile, like the anticipation of an early morning flight to go on vacation. (Or being woken up by your older brother on Christmas Eve in 1965 because he heard Santa Claus on the roof, and having both of us run to the front window and SEEING Santa's sleigh flying over the Thompson's house across the street. That did happen, and to this day, we would both gladly take a lie detector test to prove it!) Anyway, this was one of those nights. We got up at regular intervals to go outside in the dark to watch and photograph trains. Lots and lots of trains. It was a fun and memorable night.

Breakfast on Saturday morning consisted of the first of many Captain and Diet Cokes of what would turn out to be a very long day. My brand new iPhone was fully charged and ready for a full day of pictures and videos documenting our travels. I had just pur-chased the iPhone less than a week before the trip, at a cost of exactly 16 dollars more than my mortgage payment, and was eager to put it through its high-tech paces.

My previous phone had been one of the original flip phones, complete with T9 texting technology. The T in T9 stood for "text," and the 9 stood for the number of times you cursed trying to spell out simple words. Actually, T9 stood for "text on nine keys." It was how you sent a text on a phone before they came equipped with full keyboards. For example, if you were going to start a text to your friend named Michael with his name, you would press the number 6 on the phone one time for the letter "m," the number 4, three times for the letter "i," then the number 2, three times for the letter "c," and so on until you realized it was actually faster to get in your car and drive to Michael's house and deliver the message in person. T9 used predictive text to try to guess the word you were spelling. Again, texting Michael, after spelling out the first three letters "M-I-C," the predictive text may have filled in the rest with "mice," or "Michelin," or "microphone," etc. It made for some hysterical texts.

Since the Desperado roller coaster did not open until later in the day, we packed up the rental car with Mark in the backseat, Tom behind the wheel, and me riding shotgun, and headed down Route 15 toward Death Valley and the town of Baker to see the world's largest working thermometer. Because, well … why not. The 45-minute drive to Baker was scenic and filled with the kind of jokes and humor that, if repeated in the average workplace, would result in a memo from the HR department. In other words, it was a short, fun drive. Tom got us there safely and on time, which was noteworthy for Tom. I have been on road trips with Tom in which he said something like, "Hey, there's a great place for breakfast that we should try, it's only a couple of hours from here." And by a couple, he meant 4 or 5. The fact that we were at the world's tallest working thermometer before 10:00 in the morning was some sort of record.

The thermometer was cool! It is 134 feet tall and can display temperatures up to 134 degrees Fahrenheit, which commemorates the highest temperature ever recorded in Death Valley way back in 1913. It fell into disrepair years after our visit but has since been restored and worth the trip for fans of Americana. We all took turns taking pictures in front of it, and then headed into the Bun Boy restaurant for some non-liquid nutrition to offset the early morning and ill-advised Captain and Diet Coke. Life lessons.

Having our fill of food and sightseeing, we climbed back into the rental car and headed back on Route 15, the next scheduled stop being Primm Valley and the Desperado roller coaster. Although it was only mid-April, the temperature in the desert had already passed the 80-degree mark by 11:00. I do love the landscape of the desert southwest. Back home in Central New York, I'm used to seeing rolling hills, colorful farm fields, and dollar stores. However, due to CNY's geographic location southeast of Lake Ontario, with the prevailing northwest winds and lake effect clouds, the skies are often the color of battleship gray. The intense desert sunshine and surrounding mountains were a welcome change.

The Desperado roller coaster sticks out on the horizon like an oil derrick or some kind of industrial facility that is visible from many miles away, which builds the anticipation even more. Over the years, I have ridden some of the great roller coasters in America and Canada. The list includes the legendary wooden "Mean Streak" and the "Magnum XL" at Cedar Point in Ohio, the "Rebel Yell" at King's Dominion in Virginia, the "Incredible Hulk" at Universal Studios in Orlando, the Aerosmith-themed "Rock n' Roller Coaster at Walt Disney World, and the "Vortex" at Canada's Wonderland just outside of Toronto. There are so many great coasters throughout North America. A good roller coaster should make you feel a combination of euphoria, excitement, and a little dizziness. This is also how I imagine you would feel if you spent time aboard the tour bus of Guns N' Roses. And now, I was about to add the legendary Desperado to the list.

Tom parked the rental car, and we walked quickly, almost ran, into and through the casino to the entrance of the Desperado. At first glance, we seemed to be in luck. No line at all! However, as we approached the entrance, we saw the reason there was nobody in line. "The Desperado opens at 12:00." It was only 11:30. Son of a … D'oh! The only thing to do was what most every guy does when there is a sudden delay or unexpected wait of some kind. Find a bar.

History is filled with examples of this typically male behavior. The Founding Fathers met and drafted the Declaration of

Independence at a bar. (Side note, it was also written on hemp, which is cool.) There is also a theory put forth by an expert, and by expert I mean someone on Facebook, that the main reason it took Moses 40 years to find the Promised Land was that the route he took had numerous bars along the way. So, we waited, and when I say waited, I mean we had another cocktail or two.

And then, it was noon. A casino employee removed the chain blocking the entrance to the Desperado. Mark and I headed straight for the entrance like we were trying to buy the last rolls of toilet paper during the pandemic. Tom, who was not a big fan of these types of attractions, remained seated at the bar, similar to the way Marlin Perkins often preferred the safety of the studio while his partner Jim wrestled alligators on *Mutual of Omaha's Wild Kingdom*. He said he would save our barstools, a true American hero. Mark and I scurried up the platform, bought our tickets, and climbed aboard. After years of reading about the Desperado, I was finally ready to ride the legendary hyper-coaster.

Anticipation grew as the cars slowly climbed the first impressive incline up to a height of one hundred feet, offering a spectacular view of the desert on the Nevada/California border. Over the top, then a slight turn to the left, and the rest was a blur. Unbelievably fast, the kind of ride that causes your eyes to tear up, and produces screams from fellow riders.

When the coaster finally came to a stop back inside the main building, Mark and I high-fived each other, stood up, and, as I habitually do, checked for everything. Watch, check. Wallet, check. Sunglasses, check. Phone. Uh oh. Phone?! I could not locate my new iPhone! I started patting all of the pockets in my cargo shorts. I own several pairs of cargo shorts and have often magically found long-lost items in one of the many pockets. For example, half-used chapsticks from years ago, gas station receipts, business cards, scratch-off lottery tickets, etc. I'm convinced Houdini secretly wore cargo shorts. Unfortunately, no cell phone.

My brand new iPhone, which I had purchased a little over a

week before the trip, was missing. The only pictures on it were from this trip to the desert. When I bought the phone, the salesperson asked, "Do you want to buy the insurance plan for the phone?" "Of course not," was my reply. "Those plans are a complete ripoff."

Frantically, I checked the roller coaster car, the ground, the kid in front of me, the tracks underneath the coaster, no phone! The Desperado had eaten my brand new iPhone 4. The college-aged guy working the ride saw me searching like a squirrel trying to remember where he buried his acorn, grabbed the microphone of the PA system for the ride, and said, "The ride is now over, please check for your personal belongings and exit to the left."

I approached his little sound booth and asked, "Excuse me, but I lost my phone on the ride. Can I continue looking for it?"

"No, you have to exit. We pick up lost items and bring them down to lost and found. You can check there in about 45 minutes," he replied.

45 minutes?! The sudden and tragic loss of my brand new iPhone, combined with the Captain and Diet Coke, sent the conspiracy part of my brain, which is slightly larger than the "where's my wallet" part of my brain, into overdrive. The conspiracy part of my brain is actually faster than the Desperado. Forty-five minutes is more than enough time for an experienced hacker to find my phone, crack the security code, steal my recent photo of the world's largest working thermometer, and worse yet, steal all of the phone numbers in my contacts. Not to brag, but after years of meeting people and scheduling interviews for the radio show I have the personal numbers of people like the guy who provides the voice for *Sponge Bob Square Pants*, the guy who played "Big Pussy" on *The Sopranos*, the late "Soupy Sales," three of the four acting Baldwin brothers, and Brad Pitt's brother Doug. The hacker would then proceed to crank call all of my contacts, then post their numbers on the dark web to be sold to the highest bidder, allowing for endless extended car warranty robocalls. My contacts would never speak to me again.

I stomped through the exit gate, all mad at the Desperado, mad at the guy running the Desperado, mad at my friends who were trying very hard not to laugh their butts off, and mad at myself for losing my brand new iPhone 4. The fact that I actually bought a new iPhone was noteworthy. I have long resisted technology. Other than making an occasional dinner reservation under a fake name, I have never actually purchased anything online. As unfounded as it may sound, I still don't trust the process. As I have said many times on my radio show, "That's how the devil gets in your house."

Having 45 minutes to kill before checking lost and found, I dropped an audible "F-bomb," sat down at a 25 cent video poker machine, bummed a cigarette off the guy sitting next to me even though I don't smoke, ordered another Captain and Diet Coke from the waitress, and slid a 20 dollar bill into the machine. Tom and Mark did their best to calm me down while taking turns laughing at my situation as I just kept hitting the deal button. I was now beyond the loud, swearing stage of anger and had settled into the silent stage of quiet rage. Every now and then, I would turn to the guy who gave me the cigarette and just blurt out some nonsense about casinos or cell phones or whatever. I was in no mood for fun and just sat and stewed in my own smoke-filled, blue haze of misery. Forty minutes later, Tom and Mark returned, and Tom made a positive observation.

"At least something is going good for you here," pointing at the total on my video poker game. In my half-inebriated haze of agitation, I had somehow parlayed my 20 dollars into 220 dollars, which made me instantly feel better. Checking my watch, it was time to go see the lost and found guy. I cashed in my winnings and gave them to Tom.

"Take this money and don't let me spend it," I said as he carefully put the money into his pocket. We then headed to the lost and found kiosk.

"Excuse me, but did anyone happen to turn in an iPhone they found on the Desperado in the past 45 minutes?" I asked. The kid working the lost and found kiosk grabbed the cardboard box and rummaged through keys, sunglasses, and a fanny pack.

"No phones this time," he said. "I wouldn't worry too much, it probably fell out and slammed into the desert floor and smashed into tiny bits."

I stood and stared at the kid silently for a few moments. The brutal reality was beginning to sink in. Not only had I lost my brand new iPhone in less than a week, I had made the brilliant decision to decline the offer to insure it. And now, I had to somehow cancel the service on the phone out in the middle of nowhere. I bummed another cigarette off a different guy, lit it, puffed, and let out a short but barely audible string of vulgarities that would have made the director's cut of *Scarface*. My friends were silent, faces red from suppressed laughter. Mark was the first to pipe up.

"So, what do we do now?" I felt like Steve Martin at the airport car rental counter in *Planes, Trains, and Automobiles*.

"I want a new f#&%ing phone right f*@#%ing now!" Tom quickly scooted over to an information booth and asked for the location of the nearest Verizon store, and being on the border of California and Nevada, we already knew the answer. Las Vegas. The precise location we were trying to avoid on this particular weekend. A 45-minute drive back to Sin City. Forty-five minutes to further imagine, "What if the lost and found kid was wrong?" What if my new iPhone did indeed survive the tragic incident on the Desperado, and some dirtbag teenager had gotten his grubby little Skittle-stained fingers on my phone?! What if my fictitious teenage delinquent was prank calling SU basketball coach Jim Boeheim, SpongeBob SquarePants, and Brad Pitt's brother Doug right at this moment?! They would never return my calls ever again. Fortunately, I had access to my friend Captain Morgan and his partner, Diet Coke. This time, more Captain, less Diet Coke. I was so pissed.

We made the trip from Buffalo Bill's casino to the Las Vegas strip in less than an hour, just long enough to get really riled up.

The Verizon store was located just off Route 15 in a nondescript strip mall. Tom and Mark wisely let me go in first. At that moment, I was no doubt an intimidating presence, looking angry, and smelling of rum, Marlboro cigarettes, and testosterone. If chemically possible, I would have also smelled of frustration and agitation. I laser-locked with the unsuspecting saleswoman behind the counter. I'm sure she had seen my type before. Half-drunken tourists like Phil, Alan, and Stew from *The Hangover,* demanding refunds or credits or whatever. Smelling like a carny coming out of a college bar, I strode purposefully up to the counter. She could have opened up with "May I help you?" but clearly, I needed help. She went to the next level of sales service.

"HOW may I help you?" she asked. Trying really hard to appear under control, I replied by channeling Wally Cleaver's friend Eddie Haskell.

"It seems I have lost my new iPhone 4 on one of your challenging roller coasters, and I'm here inquiring about a replacement." I was proud of myself. I had handled my inquiry quite well. Tom and Mark were equally impressed. I thought I had pulled it off, but the look on her face was the same look as when my mother would meet me at the back door of our house at 2:30 in the morning, asking if I had been drinking.

"Well, let's see what we can do here. What is your phone number?" Present tense. A good sign, so I thought.

Unrelated side note, this was just the third time in my life that a woman had asked me for my phone number. My wife and I exchanged phone numbers when we started dating in 1987, so that counts. Also, a stripper at the famous "Club Super Sex" in Montreal asked me for my phone number so she could write it with a black Sharpie ink pen on some guy's bare torso during his bachelor party, hoping his fiancée would see it and be angry enough to dial it up. It was a great prank idea, although she never called.

I gave the sales associate my cell number as she clicked away at her Verizon computer. She half-asked, half-stated, "Purchased in Cicero, New York?"

"Yes!" I was starting to feel better. She continued.

"Says here you didn't sign up for the insurance on the phone."

"No. No, I didn't," I replied. And here we go.

"Well, I'm sorry, but there's not much we can do without the insurance. If you're interested in replacing it, we have the iPhone 4 here in the store for $699." My good friend Captain Morgan was the first to speak.

"Are you kidding me?! I've had the stupid thing less than a week, and you're going to charge me full price?! That's BS!" I had no ground to stand on. My argument made no sense to anyone but me.

"Well, yes," is all she could muster up. "If you'd like, there's a pawn shop across the street that usually has a ton of cell phones. You could go buy one there, then bring it back here, and I could activate it." I could feel my blood pressure going up by the second. My brain was short of oxygen thanks to borrowed cigarettes, and a little foggy courtesy of the rum and Cokes.

"Let me think about it," I blurted out through a scowl. Let me think about it is what you say when you don't have the foggiest idea what to do, like when you're getting hosed by a car salesman. Tom and Mark were of no help, more than happy to stand off to the side and enjoy my little dilemma while faking genuine concern. They were right at the brink of laughter.

How did this happen? One minute, I was having the time of my life riding the Desperado. An hour and a half later, I was contemplating going into a Las Vegas pawn shop to buy a potentially stolen iPhone to replace the one I lost while riding a roller coaster half loaded. As I was "thinking about it," the saleswoman offered another idea.

"We do have other phones available for lower costs if you're interested." Aha! A potential, honorable way out of my predicament.

"Go on," I replied with a slight nod of my head. She went on to list four less expensive options, the final one piquing my interest.

"That last one you mentioned, how much would that cost?"

She looked at her computer screen and said, "$220."

$220.00! That was exactly the amount I won playing video poker at Buffalo Bills! I called Tom over to the counter.

"Hey, give me that $220 I gave you to hold on to. I can get a new phone." Tom paused sheepishly.

"I don't have it," he said. Dead silence followed. An uncomfortable, dead silence.

"What do you mean you don't have it?! Didn't I give it to you to hold for me back at Buffalo Bill's?"

"Yes, you did," Tom replied, not looking at me.

"Then where's my dough? I can get a new phone." Tom swallowed hard, and looking out the window toward the Las Vegas strip, uttered a sentence I had never heard before.

"I took the money and bought us all tickets to see Engelbert Humperdinck tonight."

I don't swear often, but this was too much.

"Are you f$#!ing kidding me?! Why the f#%! would you do that?!"

Tom stammered, "Well, I thought we were pooling our winnings like we did last night for dinner, so when you were talking to the kid at the lost and found at Buffalo Bill's, I bought the tickets." Mark was laughing hard. I stared quietly out the window for a moment, then looked up toward the strip.

"So, which hotel has Engelbert?" I asked. Again, Tom swallowed.

"Actually, he's not performing in Las Vegas tonight," he said. "He's in Laughlin, Nevada." What the actual f#$&?! The reality had set in that I would not be getting a replacement phone. I thanked the nice lady behind the counter and started walking out of the store. I stared at my friend.

"In all these years, when have you ever heard me say, 'You know what I'd like to do tonight? Jam three guys into a rental car, drive out in the middle of nowhere in the desert, and blow my gambling winnings on tickets to see Engelbert F#*!ing Humperdinck!'"

We all got in the car, Mark was now riding shotgun, I was now in the back seat looking out of the window at hotels, then a few convenience stores and gas stations, then houses with no lawns, and finally nothing but desert in every direction.

And so, a couple of hours later, Tom, Mark, and I were sitting in a giant tent outside of a casino in Laughlin, Nevada, watching Engelbert Humperdinck perform. The tent was sold out. We were the youngest people in the audience. I was still pissed, but he was amazing. I was surprised at how many Engelbert Humperdinck songs I knew. I hated to admit it, but I had a good time.

After the show, we gambled for a little while at the Laughlin casino, and by that I mean we lost money, hopped back into the rental car, and headed back to the Nipton hotel for another night of interrupted sleep. The loud, overnight trains are fun and charming, until you lose your brand new iPhone on a rollercoaster, and money at a casino. In the morning, Tom brought up the inevitable question that I had not addressed yet.

"So, did you call Kim to tell her you lost your new phone?" followed by the kind of laugh only friends can get away with.

"Last night, I was thinking I would just tell her when I got home," I said. "But this morning, I'm thinking, just in case she was trying to get a hold of me, I should just rip the Band-Aid off, call her from here, and tell her."

"Good call," Tom said. "You can use my phone."

I took his phone and strolled off towards the railroad tracks. I took a deep breath as I dialed her number, convinced she would be upset at the news that I blew a lot of money on a brand new iPhone just the week before, only to lose it on a rollercoaster in the desert. She picked up after a few rings.

"Hello?" she said as she answered.

"Hi, it's just me," I replied.

"Oh," she continued. "I didn't recognize the phone number. Is everything alright?"

I suppose I could have said something like, "My phone was

stolen at a rest stop," or, "I gave my phone to a less fortunate family whose car was broken down on the side of the road," or, "The phone was damaged in a fight with a bunch of bikers." But after knowing me since 1987, she would have instantly seen through the bad excuses, so I just blurted it out.

"I lost my new iPhone on a rollercoaster in the desert." (As they say in politics, I "redacted" information regarding any intake of booze). There was a pause just long enough to suspect dropped cell service, or worse yet, shocked silence. I started to get nervous, and just as I was about to repeat myself, came the response from the other end of the phone.

"Hahahaha! That's hysterical! And how did you manage that?" she said. Relieved, I joined in the laughter.

"I really have no idea. We got on the rollercoaster, had a great ride, and when it came to a stop, I checked everywhere. It was just gone."

"Did you have a few beers?" She knew. Busted.

"Well, we might have had one or two," I admitted. We also might have had one or two for breakfast, one or two for lunch, and one or two just because.

"When you get home, you'll have to get a new one." She added, "And this time, you're getting the insurance plan."

The call went better than my friends predicted it would. Guys like to bust on each other at times like this. I gave the phone back to Tom, all of us laughing at the entire episode. I looked at my watch, keeping an eye on the time as my flight back to Syracuse was about two hours away, and we were about an hour from the airport in Las Vegas. Mark had a great idea.

"Think we have time for a beer?" Women would have already arrived at the airport, passed through security, and made necessary phone calls. Men?

"Absolutely," Tom replied with no hesitation.

We all made it to our flights, but just barely. It was good to get home.

CHAPTER 9

EMERGENCY OIL CHANGE

I really do try to take care of myself. I don't smoke. I don't drink to excess, unless you count camping. Or hockey games. Or Trips to Canada. Like most people my age, as a young man, I went out all the time. In the late '70s and early '80s, my friends and I would go out to bars virtually every night of the week. And we stayed all night long, often closing the places down after last call at 2:00 in the morning, then going to Denny's for a Grand Slam breakfast, home in bed by 3:30, and then getting up to go to work wearing the same clothes that smelled of cigarettes because smoking indoors was still allowed. I missed the smokers when smoking was eventually banned in bars. In the back of my head, I knew that if a large fight broke out in a bar, I could probably outrun the smokers.

Needless to say, when I was in my early 20s, I was not exactly the picture of health. Although I played sports in high school, I was never what you would call a stud. I was more the fat kid who had to wear the coach's pants. As it turns out, staying out drinking until last call, overeating at 3:00 in the morning, and then going straight to bed may not have been the healthiest of choices. But it sure was fun.

At 27, I decided it was time to start taking better care of myself. At five feet eight inches tall, I weighed in at a hefty 280 pounds, about the same weight as NBA center Dwight Howard, who is nearly seven feet tall, and presumably does not put as much butter and syrup on his pancakes as I do. Naked, standing sideways, I looked like the letter Q.

Through the radio station, I was able to join one of those national weight loss programs that required weekly visits to check your progress and provide helpful diet advice. For example, they suggested that one serving of steak is roughly the size of the palm of your hand. I found this to be challenging, as I would usually eat that much steak just checking to see if it was done yet. The diet also suggested drinking 8-10 glasses of water each day. I spent more time on that diet looking for restrooms than those guys in that commercial for Flomax.

Once I got started, I became very motivated. Part of the deal with the radio station was that I had to give weekly updates on my progress in recorded commercials on the air, so that added to the pressure to succeed. In the first few weeks, I lost over 20 pounds. Overall, in the first month, I dropped a little over 30 pounds, or roughly the weight of a preschooler. While a solid start, with a beginning weight of 280 pounds, as the joke goes, that was like "throwing a deck chair off the Titanic."

About one month into my weight loss plan, I started to walk for exercise on a daily basis, 20 minutes or so to begin with, and then increasing that to an hour per day. At the time, I lived on the west side of Syracuse, and my walking route took me up the South Avery Avenue hill to Burnet Park, and then passed the Burnet Park Zoo, and finally looped back to my apartment off of Grand Avenue. The current zoo in Burnet Park is the Rosamond Gifford Zoo and is a truly world-class destination that I would recommend for anyone. Exhibits like the Asian elephant preserve and penguin coast are second to none.

The really old Burnet Park Zoo, the one I remember from school field trips as a third grader, more resembled the type of open-air animal experience one might have seen in places thought to be the source of COVID. I seem to remember random cages of rabbits and guinea pigs, and other small animals that you could pet and feed. For a kid, it was awesome. The current zoo is fantastic.

I quickly looked forward to my daily walks and slowly increased my pace to the point where I could get a good sweat going, the kind of sweat I used to get from eating too much meat. While I can't remember the exact date of my first run, I vividly remember the moment of it. I had walked to the highest point of Burnet Park near the entrance off of Coleridge Avenue and just started running. I'm pretty sure the last time I had run at all was to get ahead of a large family at the front door of a Burger King so I wouldn't get stuck behind them. I remember it felt good to run. It was not a fast run, but I ran. I ran for probably 15 or 20 minutes, mostly downhill from the park, back to my apartment.

Up until that moment, I had never understood the appeal of running on purpose. Whenever I had seen someone running for exercise, they were never smiling. In fact, many runners look downright mad. But now I understood the effort and the reward, so it felt good. So, I started running.

Between the weight loss program and the running, I eventually lost close to a hundred pounds, roughly the weight of a decent-sized digital piano. I felt great and looked like a new person. Although over the years my weight would fluctuate up and down as much as 25 pounds, I've kept up the running and have been able to at least manage the pounds. I agree that it's important to take care of yourself. I also believe life is short, so go ahead and eat the cookie.

Running has many documented health benefits, including weight loss, lowering of blood pressure, and improvement of mental health, just to name a few. Running also acts as a natural laxative, often working within minutes. I was in New York City many years ago with my radio partners, Dave Coombs and Lisa Chelenza, to broadcast our morning show on TK99 from the Big East basketball tournament. One morning after the show, I went back to my room at the Marriott East Side, changed into my running gear, and then made my way to Central Park. I crossed 58th Street in front of the Plaza Hotel and started my run. At this point, I should define my running pace as slightly faster than walking up the aisle in church to take communion, but not quite as fast as rushing to the bar at last call. I run for the fresh air, sunshine, and the extra beer I might treat myself to afterwards.

I ran the full loop in Central Park, a gorgeous run of about six miles, and for the record, I witnessed zero muggings. I exited the park at the corner of 59th Street and 5th Avenue, and as I walked across the intersection for my cooldown, the natural laxative effect of the run began to kick in, and by that, I mean the countdown had begun. T-minus maybe 60 seconds until the main rocket boosters would begin the launch process. Fortunately, the front entrance to the Plaza Hotel was just a few steps away. I will spare the details, but suffice to say the restrooms off the main lobby of the Plaza Hotel are clean and accommodating. Maybe it was the combination of the run, late nights, and restaurant food, but that was just the beginning. On that morning in New York City, on my way back to the Marriott East Side from Central Park after a six-mile run, I had to stop and use the bathrooms in the lobbies of the Plaza Hotel, Trump Towers, and the Waldorf Astoria. It was a rare "Gordie Howe hat trick" of upscale toilets that, to my knowledge, has yet to be repeated.

A favorite running spot in the Syracuse area is the beautiful Onondaga Lake Park. Onondaga Lake once had the distinction of being named the most polluted inland body of water in the United States. Through various cleanup efforts over the years, the lake has made a wonderful comeback and is now a great spot for boating and fishing. However, there was a time not that long ago when the aroma near the lake would make your eyes water. On a hot summer day with no breeze, the lake would smell like a cross between a massive Styrofoam fire and feet. It is much better now, and there is an awesome trail system around most of the lake that is great for walking, running, bicycling, or stepping on goose poop.

One September day, I drove to the park after getting off the air, and went on a nice, long run of about seven miles. After a brief cool-down walk, and right on schedule, the near-instant cleansing effect of a long run began its process. I didn't panic as there are public restrooms scattered throughout the beautiful park. I casually but quickly made my way to the door of the nearest restroom, reached out to grab the handle, gave it a tug, and … no go. The door was locked, and a little sign to the right of the door explained that the restroom would be closed while it was being renovated. Renovated?! Uh-oh. An unexpected speed bump. I took a deep breath and thought of the next closest restroom in the park, just a short walk away. I didn't even get all the way to the building when I saw the "Under Repair" sign on the door. Strike two.

I made it back to the car via a shortcut through a family picnic, waving the universal "sorry" wave, and smiling the "my bad" grin to the gathering. It wasn't quite an emergency yet, but if this were international diplomacy, NORAD would have been alerted. I felt a little better after I got to my car and thought I could probably make it home, so off I went to snake my way through the neighborhoods of Liverpool toward North Syracuse, and eventually back to Cicero and the comfort of my own Kohler commode, which by the way has a nice view of the woods across the street.

A sudden gurgle rumbled deep, and suddenly my plans had to change. It had become obvious that making it all the way back home was no longer going to be an option. I suppose I could have tried, but if I was wrong, the unfortunate bathroom accident en route would have resulted in an expensive cleanup and, quite possibly, the sale of that car. It was time to make an executive decision. I swung into a convenience store and made a mad dash to the men's room. As it turned out, it was a one-seater and it was occupied. Again, if NORAD had been notified, we would have been at DEFCON 3 … "increased regional tension."

I scrambled back to the car, headed down Taft Road, and through what I swear was a yellow light, and into the parking lot of a CVS drug store. The automatic doors squeaked open as I walked through the crowded store at a pace that equaled the actual speed of my run, like Olympic race walking but with no medal at the finish line. As I turned the corner at the pharmacy, anxiety kicked in as there was a line for the bathroom. There were two older gentlemen waiting patiently, and I'm pretty sure I could have taken them both at once, but now I was sweating and in danger of being the source of the dreaded "clean up in aisle two."

I waddled at a quick pace back to my car and started to consider the unthinkable. For the second time in my adult life, I might have to give up, let nature take its own course right there in my car, and drive home sitting in my own befoulment. (The first time involved a college graduation party and a dare. Don't judge me.) I was now at DEFCON 2, shivering in my car and still at least 15 minutes from my house.

At this point, I wasn't even wearing a seatbelt due to the added pressure on my midsection, and just in case I had to exit my car in a hurry. Just as I was ready to throw in the towel that I wish I actually had at that moment, there was a glimmer of hope. As it turned out there was a Jiffy Lube oil change place on the left hand side of the road with no oncoming traffic from the opposite direction, so I made a quick left turn with no turn signal, drove into the parking lot, jumped out of my car, ran into the waiting room of the Jiffy Lube and straight to the bathroom. Suddenly, I heard a voice from behind the service counter.

"Restrooms are for customers only." At that point, I was squinting, gurgling, sweating, getting lightheaded, and about to spontaneously combust like the drummer in *Spinal Tap*. But I held it together, nodded, retrieved my car keys from my pocket, and tossed them to the Jiffy Lube guy. I managed enough composure to blurt out my request.

"Oil change and lube, please." At that point, if he had said I needed a complete engine overhaul, new brakes, and a transmission, I would have said, "Go ahead, do it."

The bottom line is that I didn't have an accident in my car, I got my oil changed even though I didn't really need one yet, the Jiffy Lube guy got a new customer, and thankfully, the fan in the men's room was working. As pilots are fond of saying, any landing you can walk away from is a good one.

CHAPTER 10

VEGAS BABY!

In the fall of 2003, a new budget airline came to Syracuse Hancock International Airport. For the record, actual international travel from the Syracuse Airport is much like any real multicultural food served at the International House of Pancakes. Very limited. As much as I love a good IHOP, I don't believe it truly represents Italian, French, Asian, or any other international cuisine. I doubt that if I traveled to Rome, Paris, or any of the fine cities of Europe, I could find an IHOP. However, I believe if Europeans were to try an IHOP pancake combo, they would instantly change their minds, and IHOPs would pop up near the Eiffel Tower, Buckingham Palace, and quite possibly the Vatican. I think the Syracuse Airport has flights to Toronto and Ottawa, and has border agents nearby, and therefore counts as an international airport.

There seem to be countless budget airlines that come and go, operating for a few years before going belly up. They suck you in with unbelievable travel deals, like $79 tickets to Florida that sound too good to be true. Here's how it works. You see a great deal on a low-cost, budget airline called something like Beach Sand Airlines, you find a $79 ticket, buy it, and then read the fine print. "One way only, does not include a return trip, does not include the baggage fee of $100 per bag, does not include destination fee, ground transportation fee, undisclosed Canadian Provincial taxes even though the flight goes nowhere near Canada, the local and federal taxes of every state Beach Sand Airlines flies over, and may not even include the price of the actual ticket as the purchase makes no guarantee that you'll get on this plane." And suddenly, that $79 bargain ticket is somehow $540.99, with onboard safety instructions available for an additional fee.

TransMeridian Airlines was one of those types of budget operations. They announced an amazing direct, non-stop flight from Syracuse Hancock International Airport to McCarran International Airport in Las Vegas. The flight was to be twice a week. Being direct, the plane left Syracuse on Friday morning at 9:00, and with the non-stop flight combined with time zone changes, it somehow arrived in Las Vegas at 11:00 in the morning, essentially giving the traveler an extra day to blow their money in Sin City. Prior to the direct, non-stop flight, flying to Las Vegas was a chore. You'd hop on a plane in Syracuse at say 4:00 PM on a Friday, fly to Pittsburgh, or Chicago, or Cincinnati for a two or more hour layover, get back on a plane for another two or three hours, and between the flight and time zone changes, you would somehow arrive in Las Vegas a week later. At least that's what it felt like. Actually, it might be around 11:00 PM. Anyway, the point is that a direct, non-stop flight to Las Vegas was awesome.

Our radio station partnered up with TransMeridian to do a promotion where I would accompany 20 of our listeners on the flight to Las Vegas on a Friday, spend three nights, and return to Syracuse. We would give away the seats on the flight, and then listeners would book their own hotel room wherever they wanted to stay. It was a great radio promotion, and I live for free travel.

Every Saturday morning for several years, I would meet a group of friends for breakfast at a local diner. When everyone showed up, it was a pretty good-sized group, maybe 8 or 10 friends. There was a smaller core group that was there every week. The New York

Yankees may have had their "core four," but they would not have stacked up with my core four, which consisted of my friends Mike Goss, "Moose," Joe Peluso, and me. Combined, we're looking at one heart attack, a stroke, dialysis, several statins and blood pressure medications, a borderline gambling problem, two Buicks, one walker, and a lifetime of stories and laughs. I miss all of them. Mike was a longtime comedy friend and one of the funniest, with perhaps the most dynamic presence onstage of anyone I have ever known. "Moose," whose real name was Tom, was a retired steelworker. Joe was retired from something, but I never actually knew where he was retired from. All three were old-school northsiders with amazing local stories. Those were some great times, with breakfast often lasting well past lunch. I arrived at "Pete's Rise 'n Shine" diner on the Saturday after the radio station promotion was announced, and Moose piped up with his solid 'nort side dialect.

"We're going to Las Vegas wit youse guys on your trip," he declared. I was definitely surprised.

"Who's we?" I asked. Moose replied with a devilish smile.

"Me and Joe. We got two tickets on that flight to Vegas."

"Oh," I responded. "That's awesome. Where are youse guys going to be staying in Vegas?" Moose smiled that childish, retired steelworker smile of his.

"Wit' you," he said.

After a few moments of what would be considered in the radio business as "dead air," I said, "Well, how am I supposed to arrange that? My room is a single and being taken care of by the radio station." Joe was ready with the answer.

"You've got plenty of time to figure that out, haha!" There are times in your life when you forget why certain people are your friends. This was one of those times.

Needless to say, when we arrived in Las Vegas, I was able to change my room at the pyramid-shaped Luxor Hotel on the Strip to have two single beds and a rollaway cot. I let Moose and Joe figure out who was going to get the bed and who was going to get the cot, which was basically Moose telling Joe, "Youse got the cot." After check-in, we did what most people do when they get to Las Vegas, meaning we walked from casino to casino, losing money at every stop, but justifying our mounting losses by sipping watered-down free cocktails. As always, we had fun, but by Las Vegas standards, it was a fairly tame first night in Sin City.

The next morning was when the real fun began. Back home in Syracuse that same day, the SU football team was playing host to the mighty Notre Dame Fighting Irish in a game at the then Carrier Dome. Notre Dame was the odds-on favorite, and in 2003, Las Vegas was the only place for legal sports betting. Joe was absolutely convinced that Syracuse was going to lose big, so he went to an ATM, withdrew $200, and bet it all on Notre Dame to win. Joe's brother fashioned himself as quite the sports handicapper and convinced Joe to place that bet. It should be noted here that Joe's brother also supplied Joe with countless horse racing tips for many years, none of which, to my knowledge, actually came in to win anything.

The football game in Syracuse kicked off at noon Eastern time, which meant a 9:00 AM start time in Las Vegas. The game was over by about 12:30 local time in Vegas, and Syracuse won by a convincing score of 38-14, meaning Joe had lost his bet. During the game, Moose and I wandered over to the sports book at Caesar's Palace, where we had planned on betting on some East Coast horse races. The weather back home was awful, with snow, wind, and rain scattered throughout the northeast. While checking for horse racing track conditions, Moose noticed that the annual Army vs. Navy football game was coming up, and the "over/under" bet was 50 points. For non-gamblers, that means the oddsmakers believed that the combined total number of points scored by both teams would add up to 50 points, and as a gambler, you could place a bet that the actual combined total would be either over 50 or under 50. Also, for non-gamblers, based solely on my experience and lack of success gambling, don't start gambling.

Anyone I know who tells me that "they win all the time" doesn't actually win all the time. If everyone who has told me over the years that after a trip to a casino they "won enough to pay for the night out," there would be no casinos in Las Vegas, or Atlantic City, or anywhere, for that matter. Don't be jealous of friends who seem to frequently get comped for dinners and overnight stays at casinos. They have paid, in the form of big gambling losses, a lot of money for what they believe to be freebies. But by all means, if they invite you for a free, comped concert or dinner at a casino, say yes.

Anyway, Moose looked at those odds and said, "If the weather is that bad in the east, then there's no way Army and Navy will score 50 combined points. We gotta bet under." That may have been the most intelligent sentence ever uttered by Moose. We both bet $100 on the under, and while we waited for the outcome of the game, we decided to check in on Joe. I pulled out my flip phone, dialed up the Luxor, and asked to be connected to the room, but no answer. Moose and I made our way back to the pyramid, stopping here and there to drop some quarters into the slot machines along the way with no luck.

We made it back to the Luxor and went up to the room to start making dinner plans. When we walked into the room, Joe was lying in one of the beds with his head propped up with pillows. He had the TV remote control in one hand and a cocktail in the other.

I asked him, "Where were you? We tried calling, but you didn't answer." Joe replied without looking away from the television.

"I'm done for the day. Youse guys can go out, I'm staying in."

"It's only 2:00 in the afternoon and we're in Vegas," I replied. "Let's gamble and eat dinner!"

Again, looking straight ahead, Joe admitted, "I lost my bet on the SU football game and my ATM will only allow me to withdraw $200 per day, so I'm done. I can't get any money until tomorrow, so I'm staying right here." Another gambling tip from his brother that didn't pay off. Moose offered assistance.

"I can loan youse a few bucks to gamble wit until tomorrow, come on, let's go." And just like the slot machines, no luck.

Moose and I left Joe with his cocktail and TV remote and headed back to Caesars Palace to play some games and check on college football scores. An occasional hit on video poker would briefly put me in the plus column, but that was always short-lived. My lack of luck at gambling is mostly my own doing. For starters, other than maybe blackjack, I don't really know how to gamble. I assume that would put me at a distinct disadvantage to those who do. The few times I've had any luck at all in a casino were at the blackjack tables, and usually from hitting on a card that no true gambler would ever hit on. I'm the type of blackjack player who takes a hit when nobody else does, and in the process, screws up the hand for everyone else. If you ever go into a casino and see me at a blackjack table, just keep moving on to the next one. You will thank me someday.

After twenty minutes or so of playing various games, Moose grabbed me and said, "The Army/Navy game is almost over, and I think we won some money!" And sure enough, the combined point total was 36 points. Moose was right, and we each won some money! To be honest, I don't remember how much. It was one of those bets that I still don't quite understand, something like you bet $100 to win $60. I just remember we were happy and wanted to celebrate with a nice steak dinner.

I'm an old school eastern guy, so for me, dinner time was always roughly when my dad came home from work around 5:00 in the evening. In Las Vegas, with tourists and gamblers coming and going at all hours of the day or night, dinner time is when you only have enough money left to eat something. If you've been to Vegas, then you've had those conversations with your friends. "Guys, I only have 40 bucks left. I can either get the buffet at Circus Circus or try to double it on the roulette wheel. What do you think?"

"Dude, you should totally let it ride, bro!" If this were happening in a high school health class video, this is where the teacher would hit pause and then offer up some life advice. "Kids, don't ever let your friends decide whether or not you should eat or gamble. You will be broke and hungry."

Moose and I knew it would be tough to get into someplace without a reservation. The restaurants at Caesars Palace were all jammed, so we grabbed a cab back to the Luxor to check the line and wait time at their steakhouse. As expected, there was a long line of people seated and standing in the restaurant waiting area, and we heard the host tell someone that it would be a 90-minute wait for a table. That's when Moose turned to me and uttered the phrase that has caused so much trouble throughout the history of guys that it should be banned.

"Watch this." Oh boy.

Moose was a big guy who looked and sounded very much like an extra from *The Sopranos*, intimidating even in his mid-60s. He approached the host stand with the best fake smile that he could muster up.

"We have a reservation under the name Gomez," he stated. Moose and the host both looked my way, and I swallowed hard. I had no idea what he was doing, and he was throwing me under the bus. The host looked carefully at his list and shook his head.

"I'm sorry, but I don't see it here anywhere," the host replied. "I can take your name and put you on the waitlist if you'd like." I silently applauded Moose's effort and was ready to agree to the waitlist, but Moose was just getting started.

"We made this reservation months ago; it must be on there somewhere," Moose blurted out. "Check it again." The guy went back to his list as Moose gave me a knowing grin. Clearly, he had pulled this before. After carefully checking all of the names for a second time, the host looked at us.

"I'm sorry, I just don't see it. You're going to have to wait." Then Moose said something that I later made him swear to never repeat to anyone. And he said it out loud to emphasize the point. Moose looked right at the guy at the host stand and, with a stern voice, made his final case for a table.

"It must be there, I'm sure I made the call," he proclaimed. "My husband and I are here to celebrate our 15th wedding anniversary."

Moose was playing the gay couple card. For the record, I have been very happily married to my wife, Kim, for over 30 years, and Moose had been widowed from his lovely wife for several years. But if this got us a table in Las Vegas, we were more than happy to go with it. If we had been an actual couple, nobody would have ever believed that I was the husband and Moose was the wife. But to paraphrase a line from a famous episode of Seinfeld, "not that there's anything wrong with it."

Again, the host looked my way. I smiled and gave a little wave as if to signal that indeed Moose and I were a couple celebrating an anniversary of some sort. In reality, we looked more like a couple that would have celebrated an anniversary in Atlantic City or Asbury Park or someplace else on the Jersey Shore. The host motioned for a colleague to step over and consult in private. After just a few seconds, he looked our way.

"We have a table for you," he reported. "Please follow the waiter into the dining room."

Holy prime rib, Batman, it worked! Moose had successfully talked our way into a packed Las Vegas steakhouse on a busy Saturday night. As we walked into the main dining area, two other restaurant staff members were putting the final touches on our table setting that was obviously put up just moments before. Other diners looked at us as if we were some high rollers getting the Vegas VIP treatment. I must applaud the waiters and staff at the Luxor Steakhouse that night. We had an absolutely amazing steak dinner and overall fun dining experience that included wine, great steaks, dessert, and a lively discussion about what gender role we each played in our newfound, but fictitious, relationship. Judging by the way Moose decided who would sleep on the rollaway cot in our room, I think I knew the answer.

After leaving the steakhouse and losing a few hands of video poker in the casino, we went back to the room to find Joe fast asleep on his cot, an empty service tray on the desk, and the TV on. Good Lord, he never left the room for the entire day. I have to admit, Joe was a man of his word.

The next day, Joe was feeling better about his gambling loss, so we all grabbed breakfast. Joe then went straight for the ATM to withdraw his daily allowance of $200. We were more low-key about gaming and just had a fun time going from casino to casino all day long playing a few games here and there, and then stopping for lunch, and then dinner later in the evening. It was a pretty uneventful day by Las Vegas standards but still a great time. Joe even won a little money at a roulette wheel in the Monte Carlo casino, which returned that silly, goofy smile to his face. The day ended, and all was right in the world.

The next morning, we all got up, showered, went downstairs for breakfast, and then went back to our room to pack for the return flight to Syracuse. All in all, we had a fun time. Downstairs, Moose and Joe wheeled their luggage out to the front of the hotel to wait for our airport shuttle, while I went to the reception desk to check out of our room.

"How was your stay?" asked the woman at the front desk.

"Great," I replied with a smile. "We all had a fun few days."

Given that my room was comped for this trip, checking out was merely a formality and should have been pretty easy, but as I was preparing to grab my bag and join the guys out in front of the hotel, the front desk woman took me by surprise.

"That will be a total of $225. Would you like to put that on your credit card?" She smiled and waited for my response.

Suddenly stunned and after a quick pause, I said, "I'm sorry, I thought the room was already paid for, I didn't realize there were other charges."

"Yes, the room was comped," she said. "But I'm showing other room charges. Would you like to see them?"

"Absolutely," as I nodded. She hit print on her computer and handed me the printout. And there it was. The list of items that Joe had charged during the day he never left the room. There was the sandwich he ordered from room service. Then he ordered two cocktails. Later, he ordered not one, but two pizzas. And seven porn movies on the adult channel. SEVEN! At $20 each! (For what it's worth, 2 notable film titles that appeared on the list were "On Golden Blond" and "Edward Penishands.") No wonder he never left the room; he was having a pizza porn party in Vegas all by himself in a hotel room that was under my name. And he never once said a word, as if no one would notice seven porn movies, pizza, and booze on the room charge like a little kid who closes his eyes and thinks nobody can see him. Who does that?! My friend Joe did that.

I settled up at the desk, on my credit card, and joined Moose and Joe in front of the hotel, and Joe piped up.

"We all good here?" I stared at Joe just long enough to make him understand that we were not all good here.

"I just had to put $225 of your porn party on my credit card to settle the bill!" Moose burst out with the loudest laugh I had heard all weekend. Joe looked surprised and said, "I thought the radio station was paying for the room."

"Yes, the room was comped by a client," I argued. "But not the porn, pizza, room service, and booze! For crying out loud, now I have to explain all that when we get back home!" Joe joined Moose in laughter. He chortled, "You gotta admit, that's pretty funny, right?"

I thought for a moment and said, "It will only be funny if nobody says anything about it." At this point, I even had to laugh.

Surprisingly, no one said a word about the extra room charges in Las Vegas. It kind of made me wish I had spent part of that day back in the room with Joe. He and Moose are gone now, and I do miss them. Loveable goofballs.

CHAPTER 11

A WIN FOR THE AGES

I am sometimes disappointed with our ancestors who settled in Central New York. If you were to look back in history, the pilgrims who came to America on the Mayflower stayed in New England for quite a while, and then at some point loaded up wagons and headed west. They were smart because they avoided the Philadelphia airport and all of its delays. If those pioneers went through Philly on their way to the California gold rush, they'd still be checking the gate for the new departure time. Nonetheless, the ambitious settlers set out to conquer the West and, for the most part, succeeded. Of course, there were a few bumps in the road, most notably the California thoroughfare known as the Donner Pass, which apparently had potholes the size of half-eaten people.

They were the good settlers. They pioneered their backsides all the way to the Rocky Mountains, and to the desert southwest, and all the way to the Pacific Ocean, eventually settling in nice, warm weather climates complete with vegetarian restaurants, many with outdoor seating. The bottom line is they were adventurous people who took big chances to start a new life. Those were the hearty New Englanders.

On the other hand, there is an excellent learning center just outside of Syracuse on Onondaga Lake known as the Great Law of

Peace Center, and formally known by locals as the Old French Fort. A sign at the educational center reports that our beloved Central New York area was settled by Canadian Jesuit priests. Canada is around an hour and a half drive from Syracuse. Really?! That's as far as they got, and then they stopped. My guess is they traveled from Canada during the warm, summer months, and said to each other something like, "Wow, they have great hot dogs and basketball, let's just stay here." My theory is that our pioneers were as good as the trailblazers who made it all the way to the West Coast; they just weren't quite as ambitious. But they were absolutely right about the hot dogs and the basketball.

People around the country are very particular and territorial about their hot dogs. I know to some people hot dogs barely count as a food item, as they are thought to contain highly processed ingredients, ranging from assorted preservatives and additives to parts of pigs associated with locker room jokes. For the record, I do read the nutrition labels on hot dogs. Sadly, I often read those labels *while* I am eating them instead of *before*. In any case, hot dogs are good. I could eat hot dogs four or five times a week.

The basketball in Syracuse is also very good. Old-school NBA fans would know that the Syracuse Nationals won the NBA championship in 1955 with Hall of Fame players like Dolph Schayes and Earl Lloyd, the first African American to play a game in the NBA. Another bit of local basketball history from that championship team was the story of team owner Danny Biasone. By 1954, the NBA was struggling, with Biasone, other team owners, and fans frustrated at the stalling game plans often used by opposing teams. They weren't tossing buckets of confetti at fans like the Harlem Globetrotters did, but the games were definitely slow and boring. Danny Biasone had an idea to speed up the game and, hopefully, lead to more scoring. It was his ingenious idea to have IRS agents and student loan officers chase players up and down the court, trying to get money from them.

Actually, as much as that may have been effective, Danny's idea was to introduce a 24-second shot clock. The idea worked, game point totals increased, and the NBA survived and thrived. There is a monument to Biasone's shot clock located in the Armory Square area of downtown Syracuse. It's a lighted shot clock that counts down from 24 down to zero, at which point local Syracuse basketball fans in the vicinity boo the imaginary player who didn't get the shot off in time. We're tough on our teams.

We have been very fortunate to have solid men's and women's college sports programs in Syracuse. The SU football program has a legendary background with many former players going on to play in the NFL, and quite a few making it to the Pro Football Hall of Fame. Growing up in the area, it was a treat to watch these guys play football inside the Carrier Dome. At the time, the Carrier Dome was the only on-campus, domed stadium in the country. My friends and I would often drive up to campus to see the cavernous stadium in various stages of construction.

One night after "Sangria Night" at one of the many bars on Marshall Street, my friend Matt and I drove up to campus in my mother's Chevy Chevette to take a closer look at the construction site. For those who may not remember, the Chevette was classified as an economy car due to its size, somewhere between a riding lawn mower and a sewing machine. It was a fine little car, and as it turned out, it fit nicely between the concrete barriers meant to keep vehicles out of the unfinished Carrier Dome. We eased our way through the large opening that would one day be the tunnel through which the football team would run onto the field from the locker room before the opening kickoff. We had a habit of staying at bars right until last call, so it was after 2:00 in the morning and dark outside. The construction site at the Dome had a few security lights on that provided just enough light to drive onto the field. I drove slowly as we took in the sights of the facility, pointing out various features of the structure like tourists on vacation. It had rained during the day, so the floor of the not-yet-covered stadium was wet and a little muddy. Feeling the small car sliding in the mud, Matt said what most every guy would say at that moment.

"I bet you could gun it and spin donuts." Challenge accepted.

I hit the gas, and the Chevette's 1.6-liter engine whined like an eggbeater as I pulled hard to the left on the steering wheel. The wheels started to spin, and then the car started to spin in a tight, left-hand donut. Fueled by Sangria, the spinning motion of the car became the funniest thing we had ever seen or done. We laughed hard as the car zoomed in circles on what would eventually be about the 40-yard line. It was pretty awesome. After a few more circles, I took my foot off the gas, straightened out the Chevette, and made our way back out through the tunnel entrance. I occasionally think of the decades of amazing games that were eventually played on that field, and the memorable moments that took place on or around that 40-yard line. Doing donuts in my mom's Chevy Chevette was right up there.

After a year and a half of construction, the first football game in the Carrier Dome was in September of 1980. The new facility ushered in a new era of sports at Syracuse University, and the following season, the lovable Dick MacPherson was hired as the new head coach of the struggling football team. I would eventually host a weekly, nighttime radio show with "Coach Mac" on our flagship station for SU football, TK99. Mac was always great for a quote. One of my favorites was his response to a question about football following a loss. "Football is like sex. All news is good news, some's better."

Coach Mac was always accompanied by his bride of nearly 60 years, the amazing Sandra. During our radio show, Coach would often enjoy an "adult beverage of moderation," meaning a cold beer. As the hour-long show progressed, Sandra would sometimes make eye contact with me, and if she felt Mac was getting a little too relaxed behind the microphone, she would give me the international sign of "please take the beer away," by making the "cut off" gesture by waving her hand in a slashing motion below her chin. That made me giggle every time she did that. They were an amazing couple. I wish everyone could have seen the way Mac adored his bride, and how his eyes twinkled like a teenager when he looked at her. Just good people.

There were so many great players at SU whom I admired. I had the opportunity to watch them play, and then years later had the good fortune to work with many of them, and become friends with a few of them outside of the radio station. I grew up watching the great Pro Football Hall of Fame running back Floyd Little when he played in the NFL with the Denver Broncos. He was one of those special athletes to watch with remarkable speed and power. My brothers and I always thought it was so cool when the announcers mentioned that he played his college football at Syracuse University.

After TK99 became the flagship radio station for SU football, Floyd became a regular guest on our morning show during the football season and an occasional fill-in cohost on the weekly nighttime show. He was always so full of energy and such a positive presence. To hear him tell stories of his legendary careers at SU and with the Denver Broncos was an amazing thrill, to say the least. The fact that he knew my name and would sometimes call me to reschedule an interview, or just to return a message from earlier in the day, was humbling. Floyd was a true gentleman, born on the 4th of July, and as a high school player from Connecticut was recruited to play for the U.S. Military Academy at West Point by none other than General Douglas MacArthur himself. To this day, Floyd remains the only 3-time All-American running back to have played for Syracuse. It was truly a sad day in Central New York when he passed away in January of 2021. He is greatly missed.

We have also been very fortunate to have solid men's and women's college basketball programs. The SU Orange men's team was led by legendary Hall of Fame head coach Jim Boeheim for 47 years. For many Central New Yorkers, Coach Boeheim had always been the head coach. It's hard to remember a time when he wasn't leading the SU basketball team. Over his amazing tenure as head coach, his teams won five Big East tournament championships, 10 Big East regular season titles, made 35 appearances in the NCAA tournament, advanced to the Sweet 16 in 20 different seasons, five Final Fours, three appearances in the title game, and won the National Championship in 2003. I had the amazing experience and pleasure of hosting a Thursday night weekly radio call-in show during the college basketball season with Coach Boeheim for the better part of 25 years.

For most of those years, we did the Thursday night radio shows from a great Italian restaurant in Syracuse called Delmonico's. The full broadcast went for two hours, from 7:00 until 9:00. The first hour, from 7 until 8, was the Syracuse University basketball network show that was broadcast locally and throughout New York State on its affiliate stations. Longtime "Voice of the Orange" Matt Park was the host for that first hour, and for the most part, it was a solid hour of knowledgeable and insightful questions from Matt and listeners, and in-depth answers from Coach Boeheim.

The second hour, from 8:00 to 9:00, was often a different story. I am a casual sports fan, not a hardcore sports fan. I go to football or basketball games with friends, have a beer or two while cheering or chatting, boo the refs if there is a bad call, and win or lose, I get in my car and go home. The outcome doesn't really affect me one way or the other. It's just a fun few hours of watching sports. Admittedly, I have made a decision whether or not to attend a sporting event based solely on the availability of a good parking spot. I have also done the classic "let's leave early to beat the traffic" maneuver. I would not have fared well hosting that first hour of the Coach Boeheim show.

I remember arriving at Delmonico's for that first Thursday night show and telling Boeheim, "Coach, I'm going to be honest, I don't really know that much about basketball, so don't expect any hardcore questions." As I recall, Coach responded, and I'm para-phrasing here, "Good."

I believe Coach Boeheim enjoyed taking a break from answering questions about his vaunted 2-3 zone defense, or being asked his thoughts on second-half foul shooting percentages. The questions and responses were all solid and insightful. Coach had frequent press conferences and media appearances throughout the long basketball season, and was asked many of those types of questions week in and week out for decades.

The second hour of the Coach's show would often include everything from travel tips to advice on good places to go fishing to where to stay at Disney World and great restaurant recommendations. Coach Boeheim is quite the foodie and knows his restaurants. One night, in a commercial break during the radio show, his phone rang. Unless the call was from family, or anything else that was urgent, the coach seldom took calls during the hour, usually letting the caller leave a voicemail message that he would retrieve after the show was over. Coach took this particular call, and for the next few minutes, I could tell he was giving directions to the person on the other end of the call.

"Head south from the golf course until you get to the first intersection, then take a left, it will be right there." Coach then giggled that silly little laugh that made his shoulders shrug up and down and then ended the call.

"Someone get lost on the way here tonight?" I asked. Coach shook his head.

"That was Nick Faldo calling from the Pebble Beach Pro Am golf tournament. He's in a car with three other golfers, and they are looking for a restaurant out there. They couldn't find it, so someone said, "Call Boeheim, I bet he knows where it is." Nick was right, Coach knew the place and the directions from Pebble Beach to the restaurant in Carmel-by-the-Sea.

One night, toward the end of the radio show, a guy called from his car on the New York State Thruway. He was driving from

Hartford, Connecticut, to Buffalo, and he happened to find the show on his car radio and had been listening for half an hour or so. He had a very good observation for Coach Boeheim.

"Hey, Coach," he began. "I'm driving to Buffalo and I've been listening to you guys for the past 30 minutes, and I gotta say you're very entertaining and funny, and I'm enjoying the show. I'm from Connecticut, so I'm a UCONN Husky fan, but I wish other basketball fans could hear this show. The only time I see you, outside of coaching during a game, is during your postgame press conferences, and to be honest, you look miserable."

Coach and I both chuckled at the comment, and then he asked the caller, "What do you do for a living?"

"I work for an insurance company in Hartford," the caller replied. Coach continued.

"So, what is your least favorite part of your job?"

The caller replied, "Actually, what I'm doing right now. I have to travel out of town a couple of times a week, and it gets old, but it's part of the job."

Coach jumped right in, "Exactly. I don't care what you do for a living, whether you're an insurance guy, a coach, a plumber, a teacher, a lawyer, a radio guy, or whatever. There's always at least one part of the job that you just hate, and if you didn't have to do it, you wouldn't. For me, it's press conferences. I hate them. If I never had to do another one, I'd be happy. When you see me looking miserable during press conferences, that's because I AM miserable." Again, laughter.

Growing up in the area, I went to as many SU basketball games as I could and have been a fan since I was a kid, so it was an absolute thrill to have hosted that second hour with Coach Boeheim every Thursday night for all those years. There are so many great stories and memories from those shows. But the most meaningful memory from all of those years wasn't from one of the many Thursday night shows with Coach Boeheim. It was from the night of Monday, April 7, 2003.

That night is important and memorable for every Syracuse basketball fan. That was the night of the NCAA national championship game in New Orleans against the Kansas Jayhawks. In later years, we would travel with the team during the college tournament to do radio broadcasts from the team hotel or a local sports bar. That was not the case in 2003. We were doing a championship game watch party and morning show promotion called "the poor man's bracket," where listeners would supply a prize, come to the Sheraton Hotel on the SU hill, and find out which of the 64 teams they would get by pulling team names from a hat. The last person, with the eventual winning team, would win the entire table full of prizes. It was a fun promotion, and listeners loved playing along. As always, the place was packed with listeners and fans watching the national championship game.

We had a hat filled with the names of every basketball team that had made the NCAA tournament, all 64 of them. After the game started, we would call out the names of our radio contestants one at a time, and then pull out one of the team names. This would continue during timeouts and commercial breaks throughout the first half of the game until the names of the two final teams, in this case, Syracuse and Kansas, were pulled and given to those two lucky listeners. Whichever team won the game, that listener would take home the entire table of donated prizes. It was really quite a haul!

Syracuse played well as Orange freshmen Carmelo Anthony and Gerry McNamara led Coach Boeheim's team to a halftime lead of 52-43. The bar at the Sheraton erupted as the buzzer sounded, and our two listeners who were still in the running for the grand prize were happy. Some of my radio station colleagues elected to stay right there and watch the exciting second half of the game at the bar. The rest of us headed out. Those of us who still had to wake up early for work the next morning made sure to thank everybody for listening and coming out, and then waved a hearty goodnight as we left the Sheraton. Most everyone headed for their cars as it was now after 10:00, and that 4:00 alarm would be ringing soon. I headed off in another direction, toward Crouse Irving Memorial Hospital. I was going to visit my mother, who was a patient on the sixth floor, and watch the end of the National Championship basketball game with her.

My mother had been diagnosed with cancer the year before and had been battling the terrible disease with its many ups and downs. Anyone who has watched a family member fight cancer knows all too well the rough road that is traveled. Over the years, I have lost count of the number of chemotherapy and radiation treatments, surgeries, and trips to the hospital and doctors' offices that she endured. It really is a terrible disease, and like everyone else affected by it, I pray that a cure is around the corner.

The walk from the Sheraton Hotel to the hospital felt longer than the 10 minutes it actually took. In typical Syracuse fashion, the night of April 7th was a cold night. Many parts of the country enjoy milder spring weather than we do in Central New York, but I suppose that is part of the charm of this area. I was also thinking of my mother on the walk to the hospital, hoping she was having a relatively good day, although any day in a hospital is anything but good.

I walked into the main entrance of the hospital and waved to the familiar security guard. I had been to the hospital so many times over the past several weeks to visit my mother, many of the employees were like friends at this point. Like almost every Central New Yorker, he was watching the game.

"What's the score?" I asked. The game was early in the second half.

"We're up by seven," came the response from the guard without looking up from his small television screen. I handed him my driver's license, and he gave me a temporary visitor's pass that I slapped onto the front of my jacket, and then headed to the elevator and stepped into the empty car.

The bell rang, and the elevator door hissed open to the sixth floor. On a normal night, there was more activity on the floor, with orderlies, nurses, technicians, and doctors walking between the rooms, and family members of patients roaming the hallways, making small talk, hiding their stress behind nervous smiles. The patients on this floor, including my mother, were there because they were in rough shape from battling cancers, recovering from bad accidents, or suffering from other illnesses and diseases. This night was different.

My mother's room was at the end of the hallway on the south wing of the hospital floor, and as I walked in her direction, I couldn't help but glance into rooms with open doors and televisions on. Every patient in every room was watching the championship game. With every SU basket or great defensive play, there was audible clapping or muted cheering. At 11:00, it was late in the second half of the game, and the hallway lights were dimmed, so it was somewhat dark. As I walked, I realized the reason there seemed to be less activity on the floor was that all of the doctors and nurses were in rooms watching the game with the patients, and cheering along with them.

When I got to my mother's room, SU was up by a score of 76-70 with about three minutes left in the game, and she was sitting up in her bed with a big smile. I pulled up one of the standard-issue, solid, but uncomfortable, hospital room chairs next to her bed, and we continued watching the final few minutes of the game while commenting on the excitement of the championship. After months of questions about treatments, side effects, and doctors' appointments, it was nice to have a conversation with my mother that didn't start with something along the lines of "How are you feeling today?" or "What did the doctor say?" It was so refreshing to hear the sounds of basketball on television and the occasional cheers throughout the hospital floor, instead of the sounds of oxygen machines and the constant beeps of medical equipment and IV drips.

There were several "oohs" and "ahhs" as the game neared its

end, even a loud cuss word from somewhere down the hall when the Syracuse lead was cut to three points when the game clock showed less than a minute left. There was anxious silence when Kueth Duany missed the first of two foul shots, and one more loud "Oh no!" when Hakim Warrick missed both of his free throws with a little over 13 seconds left in the game. I looked out into the hallway and saw no one. Everybody on the floor, whether patient or health care worker, was in a room watching the end of this game. I'm sure I was not the only person in Syracuse who said a quick prayer at that moment. A win would mean so much to everyone here.

Kansas quickly inbounded the ball and crossed midcourt with about 10 seconds left in the game. After a few frantic passes, Jayhawks guard Michael Lee got the ball in the corner and looked open for an uncontested 3-point shot. As the ball left his hand, the orange blur that was Hakim Warrick flew in from out of nowhere to block the shot and send it out of bounds with about two seconds left in the game. Several screams of "Yes!" and "Woo hoo!" could be heard from various rooms on the floor. The instant replay brought more invisible yet very audible applause from throughout the floor. After a timeout to reset the game clock, the great Kansas player Kirk Heinrich got off one final shot that missed its mark and landed in the hands of Syracuse's Kueth Duany as time ran out. I cheered out loud, my mother raised her hands and laughed, and everyone on the floor was cheering and applauding. It was a great feeling!

I will always remember that night of April 7th, 2003, for what it brought to my mother, and every patient on the 6th floor of Crouse Irving Memorial Hospital, and I suspect every other hospital in Syracuse. The game was such a much-needed emotional diversion for my mom. During the championship game, there were no patients, no doctors, no nurses, no X-ray technicians, no orderlies, no security guards, and no hospital maintenance workers. For those few precious hours, there were only Syracuse University

Orange basketball fans on that hospital floor sharing that incredible moment with the team, and SU fans everywhere. For those few hours, sick people forgot about their illnesses and infections, pains and medications, and all that comes with extended hospital stays. Doctors and patients cheered as one. It was miraculous. I will always cherish that night in the hospital and will always be grateful to Coach Boeheim and his team for that gift. Final score: SU 81, Kansas 78.

CHAPTER 12

PICKLES, THE LEGEND

I have always been a fan of stand-up comedy. There is a pure, real, "LIVE without a net" feel about standing up in front of a crowd and trying to make them laugh. It is a far different experience from radio. In broadcasting, you don't know how you're doing until the ratings come out, often months later. For most of my years in the radio business, ratings were determined by complex methodology. I believe ratings were determined by multiplying the formula for nuclear fusion by the square root of pi, then dividing by the total number of hours spent arguing over which station to listen to. Ratings are important because they determine the cost of advertising on a particular radio station. Households were asked to track their listening habits for a week and then mail the paperwork back to the survey company.

Once there, the survey company bean counters would then assemble all the numbers into official-looking rows and columns filled with decimal points and percentages, neatly packaged, and sell them back to the radio stations. The day the ratings "book" arrived was always a big day at the radio station. Before the entire staff had a chance to look at the numbers and rankings, the program and general managers would use intricate mathematical formulas to show that, somehow, we were always number one. Radio ratings were a scientific marvel, perhaps invented by the same guy who came up with the tax code for rich people.

In stand-up comedy, you get your report card immediately. You could bomb on the radio, and you wouldn't know about it for several months. When you bomb onstage, you know about it instantly, and it can be painful. Through the radio station, I was once asked to introduce the legendary band America onstage at the New York State Fair. I took the opportunity to tell a few jokes, and it was just awful. A few thousand people and no laughs at all. As seasoned comics like to say, I ate it big time. I did what every self-respecting comic would do in that situation: I bailed. And brought up the headliner.

"Let's hear it for America!" As I made my way backstage, I literally bumped into the band as they were making their way to the stage. When we were face-to-face, Gerry Beckley of the band stopped me, and said very sarcastically, "Hey. Thanks for stokin' 'em up."

That was more typical of the comedy shows I did, and continue to do. I enjoy doing live comedy. I have done tons of one-nighters in small towns at fire halls, VFWs, hotel conference rooms, sports bars, old theaters, even one in a guy's living room. I remember doing a comedy show at a ski lodge in central New York in front of a crowd of two. And that's only the second smallest crowd I've ever performed for. I did a summertime Thursday night show in Alexandria Bay, New York, in front of an announced crowd of zero. Zilch. Nada. I was with my comedy buddies Steven Rogers and Tom Anzalone. The show was scheduled to begin at 8:00, and at 8:10, there were no people in the audience. Zero.

"Let's get outta here," I said to the guys. "I have to get up early." Tom was adamant, though.

"Not yet! Let me see if I can get some people in from outside." Tom went outside to the parking lot and, in a not-so-subtle way, announced to whoever was out there, "Hey, everybody, come inside! We have a live comedy show starting in 10 minutes!" Showbiz.

A few minutes later, a couple came in and sat down. They had no idea what was going on. After a brief explanation from Tom about the comedy show, the husband decided to go upstairs to their room for the night; he was not the least bit interested. His wife decided to have a drink and stay for the show. A crowd of one. She laughed; we somehow got paid. Eventually, another unsuspecting couple wandered into the bar and ended up staying for the rest of the show. The life and times of a comic.

There were so many shows like this. I did many of these shows with my dear friend, the late Mike Goss. I first met Mike when he was a guest on Big Mike's "Y Morning Big Show" on Y94. He occasionally stopped in for some laughs and local humor. Goss was a giant of a man with a heart of gold and an unbelievable sense of humor. He had the ability to command a room like no one I've ever seen and could hold the attention of the crowd for a solid two hours. Mike was also very generous, as he would encourage guys to get onstage and allow other comics to open for him. He put together a string of legendary Wednesday night comedy shows at the Spaghetti Warehouse in Syracuse for several years.

Mike would also book the occasional out-of-town, one-nighter gigs, sometimes overnighters that would include a room at one of the finest resorts in the area, often with names like Hank's Motor Lodge or Edgar's Sleepwell Inn. For this particular gig, Mike asked me if I wanted to open for him at a show in Philadelphia at an Italian restaurant hosting a comedy night. Two shows! Mike teased me with pay for the night.

"I can get you 75 dollars for each show." For me, 150 dollars for doing comedy was like hitting a scratch-off lottery ticket for … well, 150 dollars. Plus, I love driving, and the trip from Syracuse to Philadelphia is about a four-hour drive. It's around five hours if you stop in Pennsylvania to buy fireworks. Two shows for Mike as a headliner were a pretty decent payday for him, so we booked the gig. I drove my red Jeep over to Mike's house on the northside of Syracuse, and jumped into Mike's classic, big, old guy Buick and hit the road around one o'clock for the Saturday night comedy show in Philly.

Ask any comic and they'll recount endless stories of being on the road with their comedy buddies. Often, the long road trips are more fun and have more laughs than the actual gig. This was no different as Mike and I talked and laughed the entire trip, arriving at the Italian restaurant in plenty of time for the first of the two scheduled shows. We went in the front door and were immediately met by the local guy who had booked the show, an eccentric guy who went by the name of "Pickles."

"Hey guys, thanks for driving down," he began. "Follow me, I've got a table for youse guys." He spoke in the familiar vernacular of da' nort side of Syracuse, with the very recognizable Philadelphia accent thrown in. Pickles was definitely quite a character. He sat us down at our little table and, after a few pleasantries, cleared his throat before breaking the news.

"Well, guys, I got good news and some bad news. The good news is that the first show is sold out. The bad news is the second show didn't sell very well, and I had to cancel it, so just one show tonight."

I was only mildly disappointed having my pay cut in half for the night, back to 75 dollars, but Mike was far more upset.

"Oh man, Pickles, why didn't you call me before we left? I could have made more money for the night doing a show back in Syracuse!" Pickles genuinely felt awful. He put up his hands apologetically.

"Look, guys, I feel terrible about this," he explained. "I can treat you guys to dinner before the show, and I promise to take care of you after the show." He then held up his right hand with his fingers in the "scout's honor" salute, although I seriously doubt that Pickles had ever been part of any organized service organization.

Then he added, "By the way, the owner didn't want to put as many tables in the party room as I was hoping for, so the show is a little lighter, but all the seats are sold." I have never worked in the restaurant business, nor have I ever booked or produced events, but that didn't sound good. After he got back up to arrange our dinners, Mike and I proceeded to vent.

"Are you f$&#ing kidding me? We drove four and a half hours to do one show in front of maybe 40 people in exchange for a plate of sauce?!" Mike was irate and cranked up. "Of all the blankety blank things, honest to God. I turned down a gig in Syracuse for tonight, we could have done that one, got paid, and gone out to Diamond Dolls on the way home." (Side note, Mike knew every bartender, waiter, waitress, restaurant owner, priest, cop, and dancer in town. If being social were an Olympic sport, Mike was Usain Bolt.)

I tried to calm Mike down.

"Remember, Pickles did say he was going to take care of us after the show, so maybe it won't be the full amount, but at least a few bucks, dinner, and some laughs."

Mike responded, and I'm paraphrasing here, "F$&#! that f#$er!" He used the F-bomb as a noun and adjective in the same sentence. But we are professionals, so the show went on.

Some of the customers who came for the dinner part of the show were running behind, so by the time we got things started, we were already later than we had hoped. After our complimentary dinners, I got up and started my set in front of 38 unhappy-looking Philadelphians. Remember when Eagles fans booed Santa Claus and pelted him with snowballs? I'm pretty sure all of those people were at this show. I proceed to hack out a solid 15 minutes of mediocre material to a smattering of laughter and applause. Then I brought up Mike, who proceeded to kill as he almost always did, for a solid one hour and fifteen minutes. He exited the small stage area in the corner of the private party room to a warm and genuine ovation. After a few minutes of greeting audience members as they left the restaurant, Pickles re-emerged.

"Guys, thanks so much. I feel awful about the canceled show. Take this," he said as he offered an envelope. "Go drive around the back of the restaurant, and I'll *take care of ya*."

I took the envelope, turned to Mike, and said, "What the hell does he mean by that? Are we getting paid for this or not?" Mike was as perplexed as I was. The envelope contained mostly air. It was filled with roughly the same amount of cash as my first communion envelope given to me by my grandmother.

"Let's go get in the car and meet him," Mike responded.

By now, it was almost 10 o'clock and dark. I don't remember the name of the restaurant, but I do remember it was in a particularly rough-looking part of Philadelphia. It reminded me of the street Clark Griswold got lost on while looking for directions in East St. Louis in the first *Vacation* movie.

I was the wheel-man, so as directed, we drove around to the back of the restaurant into a narrow alley, with the restaurant on one side, and an 8 to 10-foot-tall chain link fence with barbed wire guarding the top on the other side.

"What the hell is this?" I asked, half to myself and half to Mike.

"Just keep going slow, he's got to be back here somewhere," Mike replied. "And keep the doors locked."

I edged along slowly, deeper into the dark alleyway, until we saw the front of what looked to be a rental truck blocking the alleyway. Maybe I'd seen way too many cop movies, but this seemed like a trap to me. If someone had driven up behind us, we would have been toast. I put Mike's Buick in park but left the engine running.

"What should we do now?" I asked, my eyes never leaving the rental truck. Mike thought for a moment and said what anyone would say in our current predicament.

"Flash your headlights at him."

My first thought was, "You've got to be kidding." Flashing your headlights at another car to signal them was the most clichéd move from every spy thriller movie ever made. Then I figured, at this point, what's the difference? I did as Mike instructed and flashed my headlights 3 or 4 times, awaiting some *Close Encounters of the Third Kind* response. After a moment, sure as hell, the driver of the rental truck returned the message with three headlight flashes of his own.

"Okay, that's him," Mike said.

Again, not taking my eyes off the truck, I replied, "How do we know it's him?"

"Well, who else would be back here flashing their headlights at us?" he barked.   After a suspicious pause, I nodded and agreed.

"Exactly."

A stout figure stepped out of the driver's side and walked to the front of the rental truck, standing directly in front of his head-lights. The silhouette was definitely that of our man Pickles. He was about 5 feet 8 inches tall, with the build of a man who per-haps thought about joining a gym at some point, but never did. He looked right at us and then gave us the universal arm sign to follow him as he started for the back of his truck.

"There's not enough room for me to drive back there," I said. Mike considered this and offered his observation.

"He doesn't want you to drive back there; he wants someone to get out of the car and walk around to the back of the truck with him."

"Well, what's he got back there?" I asked nervously. Mike paused for a brief moment, turned to me, and stated a fact.

"I don't know, but it's our pay for the night, and the quicker you go get it, the faster we can get outta' here!"

"The quicker I get it?! Why does it have to be me?" We both knew the answer to that question. Although I've never been what some would call thin, next to Mike, I looked like a gymnast.

"Ok, but I'm leaving the engine running and my door open in case I have to run back and jump in the car," I said. I stepped out of the car and walked cautiously towards Pickles and his rental truck.

"Ok, come with me around the back of the truck," Pickles said while making the international hand sign to follow him. I glanced back at the Buick, hoping Mike would flash the headlights, or wildly wave his hands, or do something to signal me to run back to the car and take off. On the contrary, and clearly not concerned with my safety and well-being, Mike nodded and gave the double thumbs up to continue.

Slowly, I followed Pickles around to the back of his windowless rental van. He grabbed the handle on the overhead garage-style rear door and raised it until it stopped in the open position, and then said the two words that until that moment I had only heard in movies.

"Get in."

I looked into the darkness of the back of the rental truck and said, "I can't see anything. Why don't I follow you instead?" Admittedly, not a strong comeback, but, hey, if the Senator's daughter said that to Buffalo Bill, she may have avoided her fate in *The Silence of the Lambs.*

Pickles climbed the three or four steps into the back of the rental truck while I followed, keeping one eye on him and one on the exit. Once in the darkness of the truck, we both stopped, and although it was only for a few seconds, it felt longer. I heard Pickles fumble around for the pull cord to turn on the light, and when he finally did, I could not believe my eyes.

The back of his rental truck was jam-packed, filled to the brim with … jars of pickles. Dozens and dozens of jars of pickles. Big jars, small jars, every imaginable kind of pickle jar. Pickles everywhere. I looked in amazement around the back of his truck and figured out the origin of his nickname. His day job was delivering pickles to Philadelphia-area bars and restaurants. He finally piped up.

"I feel awful about tonight. I'll tell you what, go ahead and take anything you want," he said sheepishly.

"Excuse me?" I asked. "What do you mean, take anything?"

"Seriously, take whatever you want," Pickles said. "Grab whatever you can carry and it's yours."

I stood motionless and stared at Pickles for a few moments, just long enough to realize the jars of pickles would be our pay for the night of comedy. Pickles. Lots and lots of pickles. I did the only thing I could do at that moment in the back of a seedy rental truck late at night in the alley behind an Italian restaurant in Philadelphia. I grabbed as many jars of pickles as I could handle. Big jars, little jars, unlabeled jars, every kind of jar I could grab. I had 12 or 13 jars of pickles in both arms. I really didn't know what else to do.

I slowly stepped down from the back of the rental truck and very carefully made my way back to the still-running Buick, pickle jars clanging together in my arms. Thankfully, I had left the driver's side door open; otherwise, I would not have been able to get back in the car. I managed to open the door with my elbow and slide into the driver's seat. Mike was stunned, to say the least.

"What the hell is that?" he barked.

"The rest of our payment for tonight," I said as I placed the jars down between us on the front seat.

"Pickles." Mike replied, and I'm paraphrasing here, "Are you f$#&ing kidding me?! Pickles?!"

"Yupp." That's all I could muster up.

Pickles had returned to the driver's seat of his truck and was quickly backing up to leave the parking lot via a different exit. This was in the late 1990s, so we had no cell phone to call him and give him the business. Mike was furious.

"I can't effing believe this! We drove four and a half hours, did an hour and a half comedy show, and got paid with a car full of pickles?!" Again, all I could muster up was another, "Yuuuup."

It was now close to 10:30, and we just sat there between the barbed wire fence and the Italian restaurant in silence for a few minutes, taking it all in. Finally, and as always on a comedy road trip with Mike Goss, we burst into laughter. Loud laughter, and lots of it.

I put the Buick in reverse and backed out of the parking lot onto the street, drove to the traffic light on the corner, put on the left turn signal, and headed home. What a great memory. I miss Mike.

CHAPTER 13

CLUB GOMEZ

I started my job as a part-timer on the powerhouse radio station Y94FM in Syracuse in January of 1984. After a year at the station in the Fulton swamp with the snake problem, I reached out to the program director and asked politely, "Please, help me." He did. I drove to the downtown Syracuse studios of Y94 and WSYR for an interview with "Dr." Phil Locasio on Tuesday, January 17th. He called me back a day later on the 18th and offered me a weekend spot, asking if I was available to start that upcoming weekend.

I answered with an emphatic "yes!" and at midnight on January 20th, I did my first airshift on Y94.

I had been using the on-air name of Glenn Adams on 'KFM, so that's the name I went with on my new radio station. Almost everyone used an "air name," or a nickname. When I started at Y94, the air staff consisted of "Big" Mike Fiss, Kathy "Rockin" Rowe, "Dr." Phil Locasio, "The Lovely and Talented" Louise, "Uncle" Fred Horton, "Strike it" Rich Lauber, "Prime Time" Dave Anthony, "Digger" Denny Alexander, and "Smokin'" Joe Simpson just to name a few. "Big" Mike's "Y Morning Big Show" was a juggernaut, consistently at or near the top of the local ratings. Along with Mike, his show featured the late newsman and personality Dick Deline, whose unique and supportive laugh will always be remembered.

Local Carrier Dome legend Dennis Brogan, aka "The Dome Ranger," handled sports updates. "Traffic" Tom Paleveda, Marti Casper, Jeff Day, and "Driver" Don were added and filled out the highly successful show. Initially, I would only bump into these guys when I filled in on the overnight shift during the week. I would hang around during the morning show just to be a part of the fun.

Shortly after starting my new job, it was decided that I would also need a nickname. One afternoon, while I was just hanging around the radio station, we started to kick around a few ideas. Suggestions included "Watkins" Glenn Adams, Glenn "Grizzly" Adams, just plain G. Adams, or G.A., and a few others along those lines.

Then someone brought a classic 60s TV sitcom. "What about 'Gomez' Adams, from *The Addams Family*?" I wish I could give proper credit to whoever suggested that as a nickname, but it was a keeper. From that moment on, I would be known on the air as Glenn "Gomez" Adams. I assumed that I would use that name on the air until the program director at the time left to take another job elsewhere, which happens frequently in radio. I never did drop the Gomez. That was over 40 years ago, and I've been Glenn Gomez Adams, or just simply Gomez, ever since then. I began using the name on the overnight radio show on Y94FM.

A few months after getting the new nickname, a friend and I were driving to Massachusetts to visit friends in the mid-1980s, and we got stuck in a big traffic jam in Boston. No surprise there. Traffic jams are to Boston what injury lawyer commercials are to late-night television: totally unavoidable. We sat in bumper-to-bumper traffic for a good 2 and a half hours. On this particular road trip, I was riding shotgun, and in complete violation of road trip rules, I had control of the radio. It is generally accepted that on a road trip, the driver gets to control the music and, in some areas of the South and quite possibly North Korea, the air conditioner as well. After a lengthy debate on the topic, which took nearly the entire duration of the trip to Boston, we pulled off the

Massachusetts Turnpike and settled it like real men … side by side at a rest area urinal with a game of rock/paper/scissors.

I settled on the legendary Boston rock radio station WBCN. Being a Friday, the afternoon DJ was broadcasting his show from one of Boston's many great bars during what was then called happy hour. Many young people may never know the fun of a happy hour, as they are now illegal in several states, including Massachusetts and, quite possibly, North Korea. Generally speaking, happy hours combined cheap alcohol with most of the songs from the *Animal House* movie soundtrack.

Often, the happy hour would start early on a Friday, sometimes so early that, in fact, it may have actually been late on a Thursday. At least that's what it felt like. Happy hours were just good old-fashioned beer-drinking fun. I vividly remember going to my favorite Syracuse bar to meet some friends for happy hour at 3:00 in the afternoon, and ending up in Niagara Falls at 9:00. The Canadian side. We wanted to see the falls lit up at night, and they were spectacular. Clearly, there must have been a debate at the Canadian border as to whether or not it was a good idea to roll down the driver's car window to talk to border patrol guards and enter Ontario with six guys packed into a two-door Monte Carlo. I'm pretty sure the vote to go for it was unanimous. Happy hour.

The happy hour broadcast we were listening to on the radio sounded like a blast. You could hear the sounds of cocktail glasses clinking together, music in the background, occasional laughter, and what sounded like bells on an old-school pinball game. It sounded like a place you wanted to go to, and we wanted to find it to be a part of the crowd. However, in a city the size of Boston with its hundreds, if not thousands, of bars and restaurants, and pre-Internet with no Google or smartphones in the mid-1980s, finding the place would have taken a good chunk of the evening. Even if we heard the name of the place on the radio, neither one of us knew anything about Boston and its various neighborhoods. At one point, my friend said, "The place sounds fun. Too bad there wasn't a spot in Syracuse where you could do a happy hour show on the radio like that."

At first, I thought of the various places we went to in Syracuse on Fridays for happy hour, and there were plenty. Again, pre-cell phone, you couldn't just call or text friends to see where they were going and make a plan to meet up. Happy hour was almost like a human scavenger hunt looking for friends, and when you finally met up, it felt like you won a prize. "Hey, there they are!" The lost art of surprise. While it's always nice to see your friends, it's also great to meet new people. I don't think that happens as frequently or as organically as it used to.

"You know," I began, then paused for a moment in thought before continuing, "I think you could fake that. I bet you could make recordings of all those sounds of a happy hour bar and play them back on the radio, and just say you were there. I'll bet most people wouldn't even know the difference." He agreed as we pulled into the parking lot of the first actual bar we found in Boston. After all, it was still happy hour.

The following Monday, after returning from the weekend road trip, I went into the radio station before my overnight shift started. I was doing the midnight to 6:00 show, and I rolled in around 9:00 PM and sat down in one of the production studios to look through the vinyl sound effects library and listen to sounds I might be able to use for a fictitious on-air bar. I found plenty of sounds of drinking glasses clinking together, beer being poured, background laughter, occasional cheers of patrons watching sports on a television, and cash registers ringing. I then dubbed them onto the audio cartridges, or "carts" as they were known in broadcasting. Carts were like the 8-track tape music cartridges of the '70s and '80s, but usually only contained one song or commercial. They also sounded way better when the tape stretched and made an awesome "waaah waaah" sound on the radio. Priceless.

When I settled into the big chair in the on-air studio at midnight, I lined up my new sound effect carts, turned on the microphone, and voila … "Club Gomez" was on the air and open for business. I would play whatever songs were scheduled by the program director, but in between the songs, I played my fake bar sounds, poured imaginary cocktails, rang up the very real-sounding cash register, and had as good a time as you have in a fictitious bar. It was true old-school theater of the mind, and I had a blast.

I only "opened" Club Gomez on Thursday and Friday nights, mainly because I never asked anybody if I could do it, and I wasn't even sure if anyone in management even knew what I was doing overnight. But the show started to catch on, and before long, they wanted me to do the "Club Gomez" show every weeknight from 7:00 until midnight. A promotion! That's when the show really took off. There's an old adage that says, "It's easier to get forgiveness than permission," and that's exactly what happened here.

To be sure, the overnight shift at a radio station had its advantages. For example, you could crank up the music really loud, and nobody cared. You could show up for work in your pajamas if you wanted to. And, in theory, being on the air overnight should have been a great opportunity to sneak girls into the studio. That strategy never worked for me. During my years of doing nighttime radio, I only invited one girl into the station after hours, and she showed up pretty intoxicated. She basically wanted to use the restroom and needed a ride home. She also ate most of my Subway roast beef sandwich.

Another bonus of working the overnight shift was that I could tinker with the station's playlist without upsetting anyone. Case in point, in the early 1980s, there was an all-night diner near the radio station in downtown Syracuse. Most nights after midnight, it was an awesome spot for people-watching. It was an eclectic mix of everything from young and old grabbing a bite to eat after the bars closed, to cops getting coffee, people with no place to be, and maybe the occasional sex worker. They had great omelets. The diner, not the sex workers.

Once every other week or so, I would get a hankering for a nice, greasy Western omelet at around 2:00 in the morning. We had several songs on our playlist that were at least 7 minutes long, including Don McLean's "American Pie," the Moody Blues' "Tuesday Afternoon," and the album version of Grover Washington, Jr.'s "Just The Two of Us," to name a few. You can probably figure out where I'm going here. I would call up the diner and order my omelet to go, and if they said it would be 20 minutes, I would wait 25 just to be sure there would be no delay, and then I could grab it and go. When I felt it was the right time, I would play my "I'm leaving the building" song, which was "Suite: Judy Blue Eyes," by Crosby, Stills, and Nash. At a nifty 7 minutes and 23 seconds, it was plenty long enough for an omelet run. (For the record, the unofficial bathroom break song for most every radio DJ was the 8-minute 42-second long album version of "American Pie." I was jealous of DJs at album rock stations who had access to Iron Butterfly's 17-minute epic "In-A-Gadda-Da-Vida." I was also jealous of a former coworker who could use the bathroom during the Hall and Oates hit song, "Rich Girl," which was 2 minutes and 23 seconds long. He was a freak.)

When it was time to go get my order, I would hit the play button, the opening chords of the song started, and by the time Stephen Stills's vocals kicked in about ten seconds into the song, I would be out the back door before I heard him say he was sorry for not being fun anymore. I would run down the back stairs, out the side door that faced Clinton Square in downtown Syracuse, and then head across the street to the diner. The place always seemed busy right around 2:00 AM, and if they had the radio station on in the restaurant, and I heard the part of the song about unlocking a heart, I would know there were still about three and a half minutes left in the song. I paid, grabbed my to-go bag, and went back across Clinton Square, and then to the side door of our building. Up the stairs through the door of the radio station, through the newsroom, and into the Y studio just in time to sing along with CSN&Y at the end of the song. More often than not, I made it back in time to start the next song. Admittedly, there were a few times that I didn't make it back, so my apologies to the overnight listeners all these years later for the dead air that occasionally followed that great song.

The 7:00 to midnight time slot for "Club Gomez" was so much fun. With several coworkers around when I arrived at the radio station in the late afternoon, I would recruit people from around the office to play the parts of customers at my fictional night club and have them go into one of the production studios and record lines that I would play during the show later in the evening to make it sound as if they were there all night long. New characters were added, like in a sitcom. One coworker, my buddy Mike Pollock, would often hang in the studio for almost the entire "Club Gomez" show and lend his incredible voice talents to it. He created regular characters, such as the Club's business manager, Saul Katz. Mike remains a versatile voice actor in New York City and has done very well for himself in a very competitive industry.

Over the next several months, I would routinely get phone calls from actual bars around Central New York who would have the radio show on, listening to the shenanigans on Club Gomez. A local TV station sent a news reporter to the station to do a feature story on the area's "hottest new nightspot." The longtime owner of a very popular local tavern floated the idea of actually opening a real Club Gomez bar. If I had one regret from that time in my life and my career, it would be that I didn't pursue that thought.

One night around 11:00, I took a phone call from a very excited young lady who asked, "So where is Club Gomez? It sounds like such a fun place!" I would get questions like this from time to time, and it was usually a listener enjoying the show and calling to make a song request. I always replied in a very general way, "Oh, we're near downtown, you know, near some of the other places down here. Do you want to hear a song?" But this time it was different. She answered with great enthusiasm.

123

"No, my friends and I have been listening and we decided to come down to the club, so we hopped in my car and drove in from Central Square." Uh oh.

I paused for a moment, debating the best way to answer her question without giving away the magic trick. Since there was no way out of this without flat-out lying, I confessed.

"Well, thanks for making the trip, but to be honest, there is no actual bar called Club Gomez. It's all right here at the radio station. I am literally sitting here in the studio by myself playing sound effects and fake bar noises on the air. I am so sorry." I waited for her reply, hoping they were amused.

"What?!" came the response. "You've got to be kidding! Hang on," she said as she turned and relayed the truth to her friends. I could hear their collective responses over the phone. "No way! Come on, that's BS!" Fortunately, their comments were followed by laughter.

The girl on the phone said, "Well, now where are we supposed to go?" I asked where they were calling from, and once again, in the 1980s pre-cell phone era, she said they were calling from a pay phone that was not far from the radio station.

"You're just a couple of blocks from the radio station," I told her. "Why don't you and your friends come over, and at least I can give you a tour." I then gave her the address.

A few minutes later, I went to the back door and let the four young ladies inside. I kind of felt bad as they were all dressed up for a hot night at Club Gomez, only to learn it was all just a show. They were very good-natured about the experience. I showed them around the radio station and the main Y94 studio, the fictitious nightclub they thought they were going to. We all had a good laugh, and it was great to meet listeners in person.

After they left, I returned to the studio to finish the radio show and "close" Club Gomez for the night. I thought of the trip to Boston, and hearing the real happy hour broadcast, and remember thinking at the time that I wanted to go to that bar because it sounded like they were having so much fun. These four girls did the exact same thing, only they went the extra step and went looking for the place. I remember the conversation with my friend and telling him, "I think I can fake that, and make it sound real." Mission accomplished.

CHAPTER 14

ST. PATRICK'S PARADE DAY MASS

Syracuse, New York, is in what people from New York City would call "Upstate, New York." To New York City residents, anything north of the George Washington Bridge counts as upstate. In reality, Syracuse is a scenic four and a half hour drive from Manhattan, a bit longer if you run into road construction. And since there is always road construction, the trip always takes a bit longer. There are sections of highways in New York State that have been under construction for my entire life. I am convinced many road repair projects are either run by organized crime families or minions from the *Despicable Me* movies. The projects never seem to be anywhere near completion.

Nonetheless, Syracuse is a very diverse city. Roughly one-third of the area's population claims Irish heritage. Another third is of Italian American descent. The remaining third is a combination of German, Polish, Eastern European, Ukrainian, and maybe some Lilliputian and Hobbit thrown in there somewhere. Like many Northeast and upper Midwestern cities, we're a lovable mongrel of a town. The mix makes for great regional and international cuisine, and some wonderful cultural events. For example, take the Short Fat Guys Road Run. It's an athletic event that draws run-ners from far and wide. Notice that I didn't say athletes. A real athlete would completely spoil this event. It involves short, fat guys who run, and when I say run, I mean walk slowly, a route that takes them past, and into, several bars. The event also features refreshment areas where they can re-energize by eating Twinkies. Real Twinkies. Not the sugar-free, low-fat, Keto-friendly Twinkies. I'm talking about the old school Twinkies like the ones Sergeant Powell snacked on in the first *Die Hard* movie. It was my kind of run.

Of all of the amazing annual cultural events that take place in Central New York, the biggest would have to be the St. Patrick's Day parade. It is a day for everyone to celebrate their Irish heritage by joining thousands of revelers on the sidewalks of downtown Syracuse, and avoid stepping in various fluids, both natural and manmade. It really is a lot of fun, and, for real, is one of the larg-est St. Patrick's Day parades in the northeast. The annual Irish-themed parade starts at noon on the Saturday closest to the actual St. Patrick's Day date of March 17th, and lasts until the start of the annual Easter parade some six or eight weeks later. Actually, it's about three hours long.

Every radio station in town has taken part in the parade. It's a rite of passage for radio DJs. I have walked that parade route dozens of times, often behind the horses ridden by local law en-forcement personnel, and only stepped on a fresh road apple once. One year, a local business invited us to ride in the back of a flatbed truck while lounging in one of their hot tubs. That sounded like a good idea, given that on parade day, the weather in Syracuse could be sunny with temperatures in the 50s, or it could be cloudy and windy, with temperatures the way Leonardo DiCaprio likes his women … in the low to mid 20s. That particular parade day was absolutely freezing, so we thought we had made a great choice in going with the hot tub. My morning show partner, Dave, and I were all ready to go. We had our swimsuits on under warm robes, and we were ready to hop in. Then, our sales rep, who had made the arrangements, hit us with the bad news.

"Oh, by the way, they weren't able to get any hot water for the hot tub, and they couldn't find a generator for the heater. But at least the water is warmer than the air temperature, so you guys should be good to go." Radio salespeople could also be political spin doctors.

We weren't good to go. It was like sitting in a giant snow cone garnished with ice cubes. The sales rep wisely left early and didn't come to work the following Monday. If I had access to a leprechaun's shillelagh, I would have hit him with it.

In March of 2023, I was all set to meet some friends downtown for the parade when I got a call from the Parade Gael, Ralph Rotella, "the shoe repair man." Ralph, born in Italy, is an icon in Central New York and an old radio friend. He literally walked into the radio station on Big Mike's "Y Morning Big Show" in the mid-1980s right off the sidewalk, and Mike put him on the air. He has been coming in every Tuesday morning at 8:00 for nearly 40 years. Even though Ralph has been in America for over 50 years, I still have a hard time understanding everything he says. He once called me to ask if I wanted tickets to go see the great "Inga Bergadink." It took a few minutes to realize he was referring to the great Engelbert Humperdinck.

As the Gael of the St. Patrick's Day parade, Ralph had many events and ceremonies to attend in his honor. One special parade day event is the traditional Catholic Mass at the beautiful Cathedral of the Immaculate Conception in downtown Syracuse. The Cathedral is a spectacular church, the size and beauty of one you might see while traveling through Europe, or watching the baptism scene near the end of *The Godfather*. The parade day mass is held at 10:00 Saturday morning. Keep in mind, this is also the morning after a Friday night of pre-parade beer drinking and partying. There was a time in the not-too-distant past when I may have just been getting home when the mass began. Ralph called to ask if I would do one of the readings from the Bible during the 10:00 mass.

"Ralph, buddy, I'd really like to help out, but you know I have my parade day routine. I meet the guys downtown for beers, check out the parade for a while, then head over to the Hotel Syracuse for the party." I waited for the potential disappointment on the other end of the phone. However, Ralph surprised me.

"I've got a pocketful of beer tickets for the party at the hotel," he said. Without hesitation, I responded.

"I believe the reading is the second letter of Paul to Timothy, is it not?" Ralph knows me. He drove a hard bargain.

On parade day, I put on my Sunday best outfit, a classic black suit with a crisp, white shirt, Kelly Green St. Patrick's Day tie that I had purchased two days prior at Kohl's (using Kohl's Cash!), and shiny, black shoes. I call it my "marry 'em and bury 'em" suit, perfect for weddings and funerals. And in this case, reading scripture at a 10:00 am parade day mass.

I arrived at the Cathedral at 9:45, took my seat at 10:00, read my second letter of Paul to Timothy at 10:15, and took communion at 10:40. It was pretty standard Catholic Mass fare. For the record, I don't drink the optional wine from the gold chalice during this part of Mass. While I am aware of the significance and importance of the wine at mass, I could never get past the volunteer holding the chalice while a parishioner takes a sip, and then taking a handkerchief and wiping the rim of the cup, as if that were enough to sanitize and sterilize the vessel for the next churchgoer. (Also, for the record, I just had to Google the word handkerchief for proper spelling.)

Mass let out at around 11:00, then I changed out of my marry 'em and bury 'em suit and into proper parade garb, meaning a warm coat and green hat, and wandered over to Ralph's shoe repair shop a few blocks away to meet up with Ralph and his entourage before walking to the starting point of the parade. It really is fun marching in the Syracuse St. Patrick's Day parade. Everybody is smiling and having a good time. A parade is like an ice cream stand in that you don't go to either one if you're in a bad mood. Everyone there is already happy and about to get even happier. As a participant, you simply have to walk, smile, and wave your way through downtown. Along the way, you invariably bump into old friends you haven't seen in many years. Ralph was a rock star, a fitting selection for Parade Gael. To top it off, the parade ends right at the party at the Hotel Syracuse.

Once inside, Ralph generously distributed his pocketful of beer tickets. We enjoyed a few cold brews and snacked on some delicious parade day delectables. People danced to the traditional Irish music, and the ones who couldn't dance just sang along. Or, to put it another way, they did what they do every weekend at the pubs on Tipperary Hill, the only difference being a cover charge and a few more hugs and handshakes.

With regards to traditional Irish cuisine, I do like an occasional corned beef sandwich in the form of a Reuben, which I just found out may have actually been invented in Omaha, Nebraska, during a poker game. They are also known by their scientific name, "heart attack on a plate." While very tasty, they are not exactly the healthiest of the sandwich family. It is also interesting to note that the first known heart valve operation was performed by British surgeon Sir Henry Souttar in 1925, the same year the Reuben Sandwich was invented. Coincidence? Probably.

I also like a nice, homemade shepherd's pie. Irish stew is always a solid thumbs up. And the pub favorite called Bangers and Mash is tasty. (It sounds like a bad sitcom from the 1980s.) However, I'm not a big fan of any sort of bread pudding as it tastes nothing like bread or pudding.

A local favorite with Irish roots in Central New York is a delicious dish called salt potatoes. As I had mentioned, Syracuse has a large Irish population with generations of Irish arriving directly from Ireland, Canada, other countries, and other parts of the USA. This part of the country was also known for the many salt springs around the area. One of the methods for processing the salt brine was by boiling it in large pots or cauldrons. Syracuse was one of the country's leading salt producers for a good part of the 19th century, and the reason Syracuse is still known as "The Salt City." The Irish immigrants who worked in the salt springs would boil small potatoes in the salty brine during their lunch breaks. At some point, someone had the idea of pouring melted butter over the salted potatoes to complete the delicious treat. It is interesting to note that the first heart surgeries to take place in America also took place in the 19th century. Coincidence? Probably.

After saying my goodbyes, I left the hotel party and made my way home, walking in the back door at about 3:00 PM. In my younger days, that most likely would have been 3:00 AM. As I put my car keys on our key-shaped "key caddie" just inside the back door, Kim heard me come in and said, "Oh good, you're home early. We can go to the 4:00 Mass."

Having just returned from parade day festivities, including a full Mass, I was sure I had found a gray area in the Catholic Mass protocol. I am the corporate tax attorney of organized religion. If there is a loophole, I will find it. I was confident in my response.

"I already went to church, so I'm good to go," I said. I had kicked off my shoes and was preparing for a nice, midafternoon nap. But then, my wife replied with something I had never heard before.

"That didn't count."

Baffled, but still confident, I said, "What do you mean it didn't count?" Without missing a beat, like the ref who knew all the rules near the end of the movie *Dodgeball*," she stated, "Unless you go to Saturday Vigil Mass after 4:00, it doesn't count as going to Sunday mass for that weekend."

I briefly thought of all of the Saturday Catholic wedding services I had attended over my lifetime that had taken place anytime between, say, noon and 4:00. So did they also not count as Sunday Mass? My loophole was rapidly closing, but I remained defiant.

"Wait a minute," I said as I began my defense. "I went to mass at

10:00, I read the second letter of Paul to Timothy, I took communion, and at the end I shook hands with the Bishop. I'm pretty sure that counts, so you go on ahead. I won't be going to the 4:00 Mass."

This was met with a moment of silence. I grabbed my coat and we left for church.

CHAPTER 15

MY SPECIAL MOLE

The older I get, the more I really do try to take better care of myself, and by that, I mean at restaurants, I order sweet potato fries instead of regular french fries because someone on Instagram said they were better for you. Baby steps. I also try to get more exercise than walking to the vending machines at the radio station. At this point, I am not trying to win an Olympic medal or sign with the New York Yankees. I'm just trying not to have boobs. And be healthy.

When I turned 50 years old, I did two crazy things. (Three if you count eating a Reuben sandwich after my colonoscopy.) I went to Las Vegas and jumped off the top of the Stratosphere Hotel. It's an attraction offered to tourists who want the experience of free-falling from 1,200 feet above the desert floor, but without the mess. Let me save you some money here. What you're paying for is the buildup, the anticipation, and the first two seconds of the jump. The actual "jump" is really just a fast ride down the outside of the Stratosphere Tower from the platform at the top to the ground below, tethered to a cable and pulley. Somewhere, I have the video of the death-defying leap, but it looks more like a lifeless body being lowered from a helicopter. Here's how to save $100. Just go to the last step at the bottom of your front porch, close your eyes, and take that last step. That's really about it.

The other crazy thing I did when I turned 50 was to sign up to run a marathon. The full 26.2 miles. I ran four or five times per week for about 10 months, trained really hard, and was able to successfully complete the inaugural Empire State Marathon, and by complete, I mean I didn't die along the route. For me, calling the marathon a "race" is generous. It was more like a two-mile quick-paced start, followed by a 12-mile slow jog, then an eight-mile really slow jog, then a three-mile half-jog/half-walk, which became a half-mile straight up walk, and then finished with a half-mile sprint to try to make it look respectable at the finish line.

My wife dropped me off at the starting line of the marathon at the old P&C Stadium in Syracuse and picked me up after I crossed the finish line five hours later. I did the math. In the time it took me to run the race, she could have dropped me off in Syracuse, driven north to Alexandria Bay, taken the 2-nation lunch cruise on the St. Lawrence River with Uncle Sam Boat Tours, and then driven back to Syracuse in time to pick me up.

I also started those regular and important doctors' visits and checkups recommended for those turning 50. Up until that magical age, I would normally only schedule an appointment with my doctor if, say, for example, I awoke one morning to find an arm or a leg suddenly missing. Guys are notoriously reluctant to see doctors. Most of us would rather watch *Beaches* or binge-watch every episode of *Sex in the City* than see a doctor.

I had my first appointment with a dermatologist to check my body for abnormalities or moles that could become cancerous. Over the years, some moles have gotten easier to see while others have become more difficult to detect, as one of the cruel effects of aging is that you have no hair where there used to be plenty of it, and plenty of new hair where there wasn't any before.

For my initial visit to the dermatologist, my wife suggested that I have the doctor check what I refer to as my "special mole" located in a very "intimate place." I'm sure that I can't be the only person with a mole in a special place. This specific one cannot be viewed unless you, ahem … move stuff out of the way. To quote Austin Powers, the mole is directly above and behind the "twig and berries."

I sat in the exam room wearing only the standard-issue doctor's office paper robe that opens from the back, and boxer shorts. While waiting for the dermatologist, I admired the various diplomas and certifications that adorned the walls. I believe everyone should have a certificate or diploma from the governing body of their chosen field. A cashier certification from Walmart Tech? Proudly hang that at your cash register. The dermatologist had several similar acknowledgements from institutions and consortiums from around the world.

I have also noticed over the years that many doctors, dentists, and surgeons fancy themselves as semi-professional photographers, covering their office walls with their own framed photos from their worldly travel adventures. Some are quite good. On the other hand, there is a framed photo in the lobby of my former optometrist … that is out of focus. That is one reason that he is my old optometrist.

After 10 minutes or so, the exam room door creaked open and in walked one of the nurses carrying a tablet computer, and following a few pleasantries, Amanda sat at the high-top counter, fired up the device, and started asking me some fairly standard questions.

"Any changes in medications? Any recent surgeries? Recent hospitalizations?" Then she asked another fairly common doctor's office question. "Is there anything specific that you would like the doctor to take a look at today?"

You're supposed to be honest with your medical professionals, so I responded confidently.

"Actually, there is." I stood up from my chair, moved the front of my paper robe aside, pulled down my boxer shorts, moved things out of the way, and pointed at my special mole in an intimate place.

"I'd like the doctor to take a look at this mole." She looked intently for a moment, turned back to her laptop, made a few notations, then left the room.

A few minutes later, the doctor entered the exam room and quickly, but very efficiently, did his thorough skin exam, finding nothing out of the ordinary. He then repeated the same question asked by the nurse.

"Is there anything specific you want me to look at today?" Again, I said, "Sure." I stood up, moved my paper robe out of the way, pointed at my special mole in an intimate place, and said, "I want you to take a look at this."

He took a close look with his magnifying monocle and shook his head.

"Nothing to worry about," he reported.

I got dressed, exited the exam room, and made my way to the patient desk to settle up with the business side of the office. As I stood at the desk with my insurance card in hand, the chair behind the counter swiveled around to reveal the nurse who had taken my intake information at the start of my exam. She had the telephone to her left ear, pinched in place between her shoulder and tilted head while she typed something into her desktop computer. I thought, "Wow, they really keep these nurses busy."

As she hung up the phone, she looked at me and smiled, and said nothing. She just looked at me. And kept smiling. I smiled back, not exactly sure of what was happening at the moment. I looked at her nametag, and it finally hit me. If I had an actual lightbulb above my head, it would have lit up like in a cartoon. I was absolutely sure that the young lady behind the desk could tell by the various shades of red that my face was turning, signaling the exact moment that I realized that Amanda was not a nurse. As it turned out, she was the receptionist. I had shown my testicles to the secretary.

I giggled that nervous giggle you get when something is not really funny, but the awkward silence needs to be filled. I handed her my insurance information and nervously glanced around in every direction except hers, tapping my fingertips on the countertop while she finished up my paperwork. She looked up from her computer, handed me back my insurance information and appointment card for the next visit, and offered up a reassuring smile that told me this embarrassing moment would stay right there in the doctor's office.

I smiled back, put the cards back in my wallet, and turned towards the door. As I was leaving, Amanda said, "So long for now." I stopped for a quick moment. I had been ending on-air phone calls with listeners for decades with that catchphrase, borrowed from fellow Syracuse sports broadcaster Doug Logan many years before. I half-turned my head around with a little smile and wave. I had shown my special mole in an intimate place to the receptionist, who also happened to be a long-time listener.

I left the doctor's office. Anytime I called after that, Amanda always got me in for my annual appointment. Quickly, I might add. Such is life in a small town.

CHAPTER 16

MUSIC CITY SURPRISE

It should have been a sign when my radio buddy Tom wouldn't say where we would be staying in Nashville. He wanted it to be a surprise. "Music City" has become a popular destination for our occasional weekend guy trips. On this particular two-night getaway in April of 2015, Tom, broadcast engineer Conrad, and I met up at the Nashville airport, where I once saw a member of the folk group Peter, Paul, and Mary, talking on a pay phone and crying.

As per usual, Tom was behind the wheel of the rental car, Conrad rode shotgun, and I grabbed the back seat of the sedan as we left the airport parking lot and headed out to God knows where. Tom has always fancied himself a CDL-licensed long-haul truck driver. Conrad was truly one of the best radio engineers in the country. We had all worked together at WSYR in the 1980s and early 1990s.

Trying to end the suspense of our unidentified destination, I piped up from the backseat.

"So, are we staying at the fabulous Opryland Hotel?"

Tom smiled and replied, "No way, not on this trip."

Conrad followed up, "Then is it the Hyatt down on Broadway?" The Hyatt is within walking distance of all the bars and honky tonks?" Tom shook his head.

"Not a chance, way too pricey." He continued, "I found a much better spot on Airbnb, about 15 minutes from downtown. I put the address into the GPS." Perfect. What could possibly go wrong?

We drove out of the airport parking lot, past downtown Nashville with its distinct AT&T building, also known as the "Batman" building, across the Cumberland River bridge, which offered up a great view of downtown Nashville and the river. The further we drove away from downtown on our course, the dicier the neighborhoods seemed to become. The Hyatt was looking pretty good right about now.

From the backseat, I asked, "Are you sure we're in the right area? Sometimes GPS is not accurate."

Conrad, the analytical engineer who is wired to trust the technology, nodded a guarantee from the front seat. "Absolutely," in his deadpan, monotone delivery. Conrad's demeanor never changes. He would have been a great poker player. Or a funeral director. He has always been a fantastic broadcast engineer and a great friend.

We continued en route via the trusted GPS directions: turn right, two blocks, then turn left at the traffic light, etc. Suddenly, the GPS voice piped up, "Arriving at your destination." Tom brought the car to a stop, put it in park, checked the address provided by Airbnb, and then turned the car off.

"That's it, there's the place," he proclaimed. "We're here."

Conrad and I looked out the window, looked at each other, then looked out the window again at the house we would call home for the weekend. I'd seen houses and neighborhoods like this, usually on *Cops* and *Live PD*. Houses with no mortgages, front steps that were a gamble at best, front porches with living room furniture on them, next to the occasional charcoal grill.

"Are you sure?" I implored. "Could there possibly be another street in Nashville with the same name?" Again, Tom checked the address given to him by the folks at Airbnb, Conrad checked the GPS, and they concurred.

"Yup," Tom replied excitedly. "This is definitely the place.

"Ok," I added from the backseat. "You go first, I'll cover you." I know you're not supposed to judge a book by its cover, but this book looked like the cover of a murder mystery novel.

We all exited the car, looked around the neighborhood, and then walked up to the small, one-story ranch-style home that may have been constructed to code if the house had been built in a Pennsylvania mining town in the 1890s. One of my elementary school teachers had one leg that was much shorter than the other one. We never really knew the cause, but we suspected that, being originally from Florida, she had lost a chunk of her leg to an alligator. Anyway, if she had been with us on that porch without her special right shoe with the three-inch sole that allowed her to walk with an even gait, she would have actually been able to stand and walk perfectly straight on this tilted porch.

Tom reached out and pushed the doorbell. Nothing.

"Give it a minute, maybe she's in the bathroom," Conrad said, which I suppose could have been true. Anyway, that was my hope because the other two options were that she was out, leaving us on the porch for God knows how long, or that she had been murdered inside her house.

We stood for a moment on the porch and took in the ambience. A side door opened on the next-door neighbor's house, and a woman stepped out looking very suspiciously at us as she slowly walked to the back of her long-paid-for brown sedan, opened the trunk, and casually removed an AR-15 assault style rifle. Just like that. It may have been an AK-47, or a Kalishnikov, or a whatever, I'm not an expert in automatic or semi-automatic firearms. However, I have seen all of the Jason Bourne movies enough times to identify one of those badass rifles. She held the rifle for a moment while looking at us, then slowly turned and walked back to the open side door and retreated into her house. And locked the door. Just like that. We had clearly missed the memo about the impending zombie invasion.

We all looked around, then at each other.

"Tom, she's not answering the door," said Conrad. "Maybe the doorbell isn't working. Open the screen door and knock on the front door. Loudly, please!" Tom obliged, and a few moments later, the door thankfully opened.

A pretty, dirty-blond-haired young lady smiled at three anxious-looking faces on her porch and said, "Hi! Welcome to Nashville. I'm Molly, come on in."

We followed her into her humble home, very neat and clean. It was a small, "front-to-back" design of a ranch-style home. The front door opened to the living room, which led to the dining room, and from there to the kitchen. The main bedroom was through a door behind the kitchen, and two small bedrooms were to the left of the dining room. Quaint and cute. The inside vibe betrayed the outside uneasiness.

"Let me show you boys around. There's one bedroom through those doors on the right, and one on the left with a bathroom in between them. My bedroom will be ready in a few minutes; I'm still throwing a few things in my luggage."

This was our first experience with Airbnb, so we had nothing to compare it with. I assumed this was how it worked. Someone put their home online to rent at a specific price, someone else clicked "like," or a heart, or smiley turd emoji, or whatever, and agreed to the price. Then, the traveler would show up, the owner handed the keys over to the customer, and the owner would take off somewhere for the length of the stay. Apparently, this is not normally how it is done.

Tom made the mistake of asking, "Oh, so where are you going?"

She sighed and responded sheepishly.

"Well, originally I was going to stay at my boyfriend's house this weekend, but we had an argument about it, so I'm going to pack up a few things and go to a hotel for the weekend."

Uh oh. I compare moments like this to an impending car accident down the road ahead of you on a highway. You can see it coming, but you know you can't stop it or get out of the way. Before I could intervene, or Conrad could interject, Tom stirred it up.

"Oh gosh, you shouldn't have to do that. We don't want to kick you out of your own home, do we, guys?"

Tom's question prompted a quick, blank stare from me, and three or four rapid eye blinks from Conrad. Surely, there must have been a page or two in the Airbnb handbook that addressed dilemmas like this. But, friends are friends. I responded, never leaving eye contact with Tom.

"Why, of course not. After all, it's your house. You should be able to do whatever you want with it."

Immediately, her face lit up, and her eyes relaxed. "Oh, thank you so much! That really helps me out a lot!"

I quickly did the math in my head. One bedroom in the front with one bed. Tom had a CPAP machine. Another bedroom had one queen-sized bed. Conrad is over six feet two inches tall and would need extra room. Her now off-limits bed meant that the "L" shaped couch in the living room, within sight and range of her neighbor's sniper rifle, would be my bed for the next 2 nights.

We retreated to the kitchen to have a seat and a cocktail. Although it was still early afternoon, we all needed booze. We learned that she lived for a while in Florida, where she had worked in a bar. Our hostess then moved to Nashville to pursue a music career, as most every bartender, waiter, waitress, and Uber driver in Music City had done. I have always admired those who pursued dreams, whether it be music, comedy, art, dance, or anything else that required strength of heart and passion.

"Good for you," I said.

"Do you guys want to hear one of my songs?" she asked.

After just a split-second pause, Tom responded enthusiastically, "Why sure, we'd love to!"

As our hostess retreated to her bedroom to grab her guitar, Conrad and I took out our cell phones and started googling "Nashville hotels." I still had no idea what we were paying to stay in what seemed like the Compton neighborhood of Los Angeles, but there had to be a better deal somewhere else. The Hyatt? The Hilton? The Omni? The Bates Motel? Camp Crystal Lake?

"What's wrong with this place?" Tom protested. "She seems nice, the place is pretty clean." Before we could respond, she entered the kitchen with her acoustic Taylor guitar. Eyeing our Buffalo Trace bourbon, she asked if she could have one.

"Sure thing," Tom responded. "It's happy hour, let's do a shot."

Tom poured four healthy shots, almost doubles. They were the kind of shots you would get at your favorite dive bar at Christmas, not the kind you would get at the lobby bar of the Opryland Hotel. Then, she uttered a sentence that should have sent us out the front door.

"I probably shouldn't have this after rehab, but at least it's not heroin. Cheers!"

Gulp. Well, this ought to be good. She strapped on the guitar, tuned it up, and started to play. She was actually pretty good. Her voice was very melodic as well. And then, the lyrics. Her sweet voice was in stark contrast to the dark tone of her songwriting. The song recounted dark stories of deep struggles, each line more disturbing than the previous one. We smiled when she looked our way; we side-eyed each other when she looked at her guitar. We all shared a common inner dialogue.

"What the hell were we doing here? Was her boyfriend unstable, and on his way over to continue the horrible argument we were hearing about in this song? Was her boyfriend, in fact, Ted Bundy?"

We hung out, drank bourbon, and listened to songs about ex-boyfriends who met violent and tragic ends. The songs sounded as if the lyrics were written by Stephen King. But we smiled, tapped our toes, and sipped bourbon, all the while waiting for the banana bread that was baking in the oven. This very hospitable Nashville welcome lasted a good 2 hours, but even the aroma of fresh banana bread and the sound of original music did nothing to ease the tension of our situation.

After the bread came out of the oven and the guitar was put away, our hostess grabbed her purse. "As long as I'm staying here for the weekend," she announced, "I'm going to head to the grocery store. Do you guys need anything?"

After a pause of exactly zero seconds, we said in unison, "No thanks, we're good."

As soon as she closed the door and headed to her car, we all spoke simultaneously, each of us uttering the "F" word, and correctly using it as a noun, adjective, and a verb as needed. Most of the commentary was directed at Tom, me first.

"How the hell did you end up here?! Weren't there any pictures of the place or of the neighborhood online? Don't they vet Airbnb hosts?"

"Now wait a minute," Tom replied. "It's not really that bad. It's pretty clean, she seems nice, we're not that far from downtown Nashville and the bars on Broadway. I say we give it a night, and if it's really that bad, or scary, we'll bail tomorrow and find a hotel."

He wasn't wrong. All of that was true, and the place now smelled of fresh-baked banana bread. And we had booze. Conrad and I reluctantly nodded in agreement.

"Okay, one night. We'll reassess tomorrow," Conrad said.

We grabbed our bags and settled in. Tom took the front bedroom, Conrad the adjoining room, and I set up the velour, L-shaped couch for the night. She was kind enough to supply sheets for the couch and linens for each of us. Actually, I had slept on more uncomfortable couches in friends' apartments over the years.

I was feeling better about our decision and our situation. While Tom and Conrad finished getting their beds ready, I headed into the Jack 'n Jill bathroom between their rooms and, shall we say, grabbed some reading material. After thumbing through her library of various catalogues and newsletters, I settled on an issue of Guitar magazine with Johnny Cash on the cover because, well ... who wouldn't?

Something about the address label grabbed my attention. The

subscriber's address was correct, but the name was different. I briefly thought that maybe our hostess had a roommate who had moved out or something like that. When I emerged from the Jack 'n Jill library, I casually mentioned the different name on the magazine to Tom and Conrad, who immediately did what anyone would do in that circumstance. They googled her. And all at once, they said in a somewhat shocked tone in unison, and I am paraphrasing here, "Holy S#@T!"

The new name associated with the address of the house we were renting for the weekend popped up on several different websites in the form of mugshots. As in, more than one. Multiple arrests. Oh, she worked in a few bars in Florida, alright. Allegedly, she had also robbed a few of them. She had also violently assaulted a boyfriend and had been arrested several times for buying and selling drugs. Further investigation into her real identity revealed solid prison time. And now, I would be sleeping on her couch. At least Tom and Conrad had a bedroom door they could lock.

"Well, what do we do now?" I asked. My somewhat comfortable feeling had given way to anxiety, much like on the flight from Syracuse to Nashville when the pilot came on the loudspeaker and said, "Sorry folks, it's not quite as smooth as we thought, so we're going to go ahead and turn on the fasten seat belt sign." Conrad went back to googling local hotels, but Tom remained steadfast.

"If the boyfriend shows up, I'm going through the window," I proclaimed. The other plan was to throw Conrad at him, as Conrad would be our best hope for survival. After one more shot of bourbon, we decided to ride it out for the weekend at the Airbnb home of a convicted violent felon. What could possibly go wrong?

Molly returned from the store and put away her groceries. By now, it was early evening, and we were making our dinner plans. She insisted that we try real "Nashville Hot Chicken," which I assumed, given her extensive criminal background, was stolen. As it turned out, the hot chicken is a local favorite enjoyed mainly by people with a high tolerance for gastronomic pain. We all hopped into the rental car and headed off to a small Nashville favorite hot chicken spot. Molly was right, the chicken was delicious. Great coating, smoking hot, and super tasty. The heat promised a guaranteed payback sometime on Saturday morning.

We returned to casa de meth, finished our pleasantries, and our hostess headed out for the evening. She offered up some southern hospitality.

"I know you guys didn't expect me to be staying, so if you need to use the bathroom in my bedroom, feel free," and off she went. A convicted felon had just given us permission to go through her bedroom to use her bathroom. So, like the cast of *Goonies*, we slowly opened her bedroom door to peek inside.

If she had planned on not being there for the weekend, then she was clearly a last-minute packer, as her queen-sized bed was completely covered with laundry, and various toiletries were scattered on the countertop of the bathroom vanity. There was also a full drum kit set up near the window. Conrad was the first to notice the 2 "O" rings screwed into the ceiling.

"So what do you think those are used for?" I asked, looking up at the ceiling. I'm not sure exactly how or why, but Conrad knew the answer. He responded in his deadpan manner.

"Sex swing."

I had to Google it, but yes, according to the image on the internet, it looked to be the ceiling support for something called a "sex swing," a device that would have sent me to the ER or to the chiropractor. Convicted felon, drug dealer, sex swing. I did not have any of those on my weekend travel bingo board.

We still considered getting a hotel room elsewhere, but it was getting late. Plus, the combination of bourbon and the knowledge that we were staying in the home of a convicted felon, who was also some sort of a dominatrix, was far more intriguing than spending the weekend in a room next to the elevator or ice machine at some overpriced downtown hotel. We went our separate ways for the evening, with Tom, Conrad, and me heading downtown to the bars on Broadway, and our hostess perhaps heading to meet with her parole officer.

Downtown Nashville has always been fun. I much preferred Broadway years ago, before Margaritaville types of places, chain restaurants, bar-cycles, celebrity-themed bars, and endless bachelorette parties took over. There was a unique, raw, and very real vibe about Music City. It is still a fun, clean, and mostly safe area to visit, but it now feels more like a Disney version of its authentic self.

After a few beers and honky tonks, which sounds like a country song, we made our way back to the casa d'felon and met Molly, who had just returned from her night out as well. We all sipped a whiskey or two, and then settled in for the night. Tom and Conrad retired to their comfortable beds, our hostess to her sex swing bedroom, and me to my makeshift, L-shaped velour couch. The combination of travel and whiskey made sleep easy. The neighborhood was surprisingly quiet. No sirens, gunplay, or unexpected knocks on the door. It was quite peaceful. That is, until 4:00 in the morning.

Molly was in the kitchen on the phone, trying to speak in a low, quiet tone, but based on her definition of the word "quiet," I assumed she had learned to whisper in the front row of a Van Halen concert. She hung up the phone and tiptoed through the small dining room toward the front door. As she walked by, she finally saw that I was awake, albeit in the shape of an "L" on her velour couch.

"I hope I didn't wake you," she said, no longer in a whisper.

"No," I lied. "I was just getting up to see if your neighbor was aiming her rifle in my direction." Well, that's what I wanted to say. What I actually said was, "I was just up to use the bathroom."

She stopped to put her high heels on. Yes, her red stiletto high heels, to match her short skirt, bright red lipstick, and fishnet stockings.

"I just got called into work, so I have to go for a while."

Called into work? At 4:00 in the morning? Dressed like Julia

Roberts in *Pretty Woman*? Suspicions confirmed. What do you say to a prostitute as she heads out of the house for a gig at 4:00 AM?

"Have a nice day." Have a nice day?! That's all I could muster up at the last second.

We were staying with a professional, working, in-demand Nashville call girl. And she was standing right in front of me, putting on stiletto heels. My wife would be happy and proud to know that a prostitute said to me, "I hope I didn't wake you up." Then she smiled as she opened the front door and said one of those things that you never hear when you're single.

"That couch can't be that comfortable, so if you want, you can go sleep in my bed," she added with a wink. "I'll try not to wake you when I get back." Great. We were staying with a sex worker who didn't like to bring her work home with her.

I fell back asleep, "L" shaped, and woke up with the fellas a few hours later. I shared my story of being invited into the bed of a prostitute. In the version I told them, I aggressively protested and fended off her uninvited advances to the point where I threatened to call the police. They didn't buy it. The rest of the weekend was fun, and after that first night, we really didn't have much interaction with our lovely hostess. Would we ever go back? Hell yes!

CHAPTER 17

UNFINISHED BUSINESS

In the fall of 1981, I was in my final semester at Onondaga Community College, OCC, and all set to graduate in December with my Associate in Applied Science degree from what was simply called the Radio/Television department. Obviously, 1981 was well before the internet, TikTok, Netflix, podcasts, and cell phones. It really wasn't that far removed from good, old-fashioned television through the airwaves, picked up by antennae, and having three channels to choose from. Four, if you counted the local public television station, five if you counted a station from Utica that occasionally came in kind of fuzzy, but aired more professional wrestling. It's just my opinion, but there are far too many TV channel choices today, kind of like the menu at the Cheesecake Factory. And that doesn't include the hundreds of shows and movies available on the many streaming platforms. It's impossible to keep track of all the shows.

Invariably, someone at work will ask something like, "Hey, have you seen that show *Naked Alaskan Dog-Man*? It's hysterical!"

To which I would reply, "No, what channel is that on?"

And they would answer with something along the lines of, "It's on the 'weasel tooth plus' digital channel from Animal Planet's parent company, which is a subsidiary of Procter and Gamble, and the company that makes recycling bins."

And then I would say, "No."

It was October, with December graduation just a couple of months away, when my radio professor, the beloved Vinnie Spadafora, called me into his office with a question.

"There's a radio station in Herkimer, and they're looking for a full-time guy. Are you interested?"

Here, I should point out that my general, overall philosophy in life is to say yes whenever possible. Very seldom does anything fun or memorable ever happen when you say no. Life is very much like improv theater ... never deny the premise. Once you say no to something, the scene is over, and you'll never know what might have happened to your character.

So, I said yes. Vinnie put me in contact with the program director of that station, WRMV 1420AM, "Radio of the Mohawk Valley," and I took the job. Of course, that meant that I left college without graduating, but at the time, I figured the whole point of college was to get a job in your chosen career. So, in October of 1981, I was officially a professional radio broadcaster. I was getting paid to do what I had essentially been paying to do while in college. That's how my career in broadcasting began, at a little AM radio station in Herkimer, New York, that paid slightly more than minimum wage, and no college degree needed. I'm sure it was not exactly what my high school guidance counselor would have drawn up, but it was the start of a fun and satisfying career in radio. College was in my rearview mirror.

Every now and then, over the years, I would think about not graduating from college and not having a degree. It really didn't bother me as far as employment is concerned, as having a college degree so many years into my career wouldn't have made much of a difference. Radio is different from most other fields. For example, I want my doctor to have a valid medical degree. I want the person who designs the bridges over which I drive daily to have the appropriate engineering degree. The person who delivers content over the airwaves requires only the ability to do so, which is one of the many reasons I was drawn to it. Radio is filled with stories of on-air personalities who came from entirely different backgrounds and levels of education, who went on to have long and successful careers. As my boss Ed said years ago, "Radio is a place for D students to succeed." It is also true that radio pays, at least at the start, somewhere between a convenience store cashier and a Christmas bureau volunteer.

Still, every once in a while, I would be asked about my college experience, and although I would happily reference my time in college, it started to bother me that I couldn't say that I was a college graduate. It was clearly unfinished business that someday I would address. That someday happened in January of 2016.

I was driving from the radio station in the Armory Square section of Syracuse to visit family in the village of Marcellus, about 12 miles west of Syracuse. My route on that particular day took me through the west side of the city, and more specifically, to a Dunkin' Donuts location for a road coffee. On Onondaga Hill, I hit the stoplight that happened to be at the north entrance of the OCC campus, the same entrance my friends and I used when we skipped classes to go to Coleman's Irish Pub in the area of town known as Tipperary Hill.

As I sat at the red light sipping my coffee, I noticed the electronic sign at the entrance of campus that read, "Last day to register for Spring classes is January 24th." I stared at the sign for a moment, and suddenly wondered how many classes I actually needed to earn the Associate's Degree I had given up on 35 years before. The universe answered by having the red light become a green left turn arrow that I briefly studied, before responding out loud.

"Oh, what the hell, it doesn't hurt to ask."

I made the left turn, wound my way up to OCC Drive, and found my way to the Gordon Student Center. The campus sits high on a hill overlooking the city of Syracuse and the valley below. In general, it seems the best views in most cities are from properties owned by colleges and cemeteries. On a clear day, you can see Onondaga Lake, Oneida Lake, Lake Ontario, the Seneca River, several streams, and a few big reservoirs. Perhaps there is a class offered that can explain why our water bills are so high.

I walked through the doors of the student center for the first time in 35 years and approached the help desk. The young man behind the counter greeted me with a smile.

"What can I help you with, sir?" he asked. Sir. I was already being identified as the old man on campus.

"Yes, I attended OCC a very long time ago," I replied. "I left college before graduating, so I wanted to find out what I would need to get my degree." It felt good to say that out loud.

I assumed in the years since I left the Radio/Television program that there must be so many new classes that didn't exist in 1981 that it might take me a few semesters of taking a class here and another there to finish my degree and graduate. For example, the audio editing I learned back then was done with a grease pencil and a razor blade, and now it is all done digitally.

And photography is much different. If you took pictures at a party back in the day, you had to drop the film off at a photomat store on a Monday and then pick up the developed pictures on Thursday. You would then sit in your car and flip through the developed photos, carefully removing the ones that were out of focus, and the ones of questionable content.

Now, every smartphone is also a pretty good camera, so the pictures are instant and can be deleted. It's easy to eliminate those pictures where someone was blinking, or someone had chocolate frosting on their face, or the cat had jumped on someone's lap right as the picture was taken. Unfortunately, many of those are considered to be the "bad" pictures and are deleted. In hindsight, these are actually the good, memorable pictures, and once they are deleted, they are gone forever. Often, we are left with nice, generic pictures where everybody's smile is perfect, the lighting is perfect, the angle is perfect, and these pictures are often boring as hell.

I miss those kinds of pictures and experiences. There really are no more surprises anymore, which is sad. I am a fan of the band Rush, and I was lucky to have seen them in concert twice. At one of those shows, the guy sitting next to me had logged onto a website that shows the setlists of bands on tour, so you could technically know ahead of time what songs the band would be playing, and the order in which they would be played. Where is the fun in that? I prefer to be surprised and a little excited to hear the songs as they are played in real time right there at the concert.

There are also fewer surprises when it comes to things like school closings. When I was a kid in school in the 1970s, during the winter months, you woke up, looked out the window, and if there was new snow on the ground, you quickly turned on the radio and listened to your favorite radio personality list the school closings in alphabetical order, hoping and praying that your school was somewhere on that list. At some point, when technology allowed, school closings were scrolled along the bottom of the TV screen during the local morning news. Searching for your school on the scrolling closed list was more like watching the results of the NFL draft, but it was definitely exciting.

Of course, now parents and students receive instant text messages and emails from the district superintendent announcing the closing of the school. During my early years in radio at WSYR-AM and Y94-FM in Syracuse, school closings were handled with the utmost care to ensure accuracy. And this was before most local television stations were producing their own morning news shows with school closing information, so at that time, radio was the only place to get that kind of important, up-to-date information.

Here's how it generally worked. We had a notebook with every local school district listed alphabetically, along with the name of that district's superintendent. Each superintendent had a password so that when they called the newsroom, the person who answered the phone could verify that it was a real call from a school official, and not a call from a 7th grader trying to sound old enough to close their own school. Indeed they tried. Those calls went something like this. The phone would ring in the newsroom, and then be answered by a newsperson.

"Good morning, newsroom."

Some kid trying to talk with a deep voice would then give it his best shot.

"Yes, hello. My name is Dr. Robert Snarlgrab from the Tully School District, and we're going to close today."

The newsperson would respond, "Ok, Dr. Snarlgrab, and what is your password?" Fake Dr. Snarlgrab would pause and then respond.

"Oh, the password. Yes, that's right." The phone would then get muffled by Dr. Snarlgrab, as you could clearly hear him ask his brother what he thinks the password would be. Dr. Snarlgrab would then take his hand off the phone receiver, and with his fake deep voice, relay what he believed to be the password.

"The password is 'you are a buttface.'" Dr. Snarlgrab and his brother would then laugh hysterically as he hung up the phone, off to terrorize WHEN-AM, 93Q, 95X, and every other radio station in town.

If there were only a few school closings on a given morning, it was no problem. Someone would take the call, jot down the information, then deliver it to the morning hosts and news anchors for broadcast. Pretty standard operating procedure. However, we live in Central New York, an area that receives, on average, about 120 inches of snow. For comparison, if the federal budget deficit were a hole in the ground, our snowfall could probably fill it. On mornings like that, with snow falling at a rate of one or two inches per hour, the school closing phone in the newsroom would start ringing at 5:00 in the morning, then ring continuously for the next few hours.

We were always lucky enough to have some pretty good part-timers working for the radio stations, but they were often local college students who were from outside of the area, and therefore not familiar with the names of local towns and school districts. On those hectic snow days, that was sometimes an issue. For example, the school districts of West Genesee and Westhill are both fine local schools. However, to a college kid from Long Island, they look similar enough to put a check mark next to one or the other, and then run it into the on-air studio to have it announced over the airwaves. There are few things worse for a radio station than inadvertently closing the wrong school district during a snowstorm. Fortunately, it rarely happened, but on the few times it did, yikes. If you've ever been outside and thought that you heard the faint sound of a far-off obscenity from an unknown source or direction, that may well have been the voice of a news anchor or morning radio host echoing from decades ago.

Anyway, back to OCC. The young man at the information booth clicked a few things into his computer, jotted down something on a Post-it note, and directed me to have a seat while he brought the note back into the offices behind the counter. Another guy, even younger than the first, came out, welcomed me back to the OCC campus, and instructed me to follow him to the Electronic Media Communications department. That was the new name of the old Radio/Television department. Right away, I thought I was screwed. I thought this may end up requiring an entire four years to complete my two-year degree. What was I getting myself into?

Upon opening the door to the EMC department, I was greeted by a familiar face. Tony Vadala, who also went to OCC and was now a professor in the department, extended his hand with a smile to greet me.

"Great to see you on campus! What are you doing here?" He probably thought I was on campus to speak to a class, which I still occasionally do.

Shaking his hand, I replied, "Well, believe it or not, I never graduated back in the day, and I'm here to find out exactly how many classes I would need to finish my degree."

"Wait right here," he responded as he disappeared into a small storage area at the back of his office. He was gone for maybe 8 or 10 seconds, not even long enough for the door to close behind him, and returned with a cardboard box.

"I believe what you're looking for is right here," he said, flipping the cardboard top off the box and setting it on the desk in front of us.

I think we go through life looking for signs from the universe, or from God, or from some higher power, that point us in the right direction. On this day, I had decided on a whim at a traffic light, directing me to turn left at an electronic sign that told me that the last day to register for classes was approaching. I found myself in the Electronic Media Communications office talking to Professor Vadala, who then produced a cardboard box filled with paperwork that he was, at that very moment, transferring into storage. When he took the lid off the box, the very first file sitting at the top of the paperwork jammed in there was my student folder, with my handwriting on the cover, from 35 years before. I still get goosebumps thinking of that precise moment.

"I'm sure everything is still there," Tony said. "Let's take a look through your student records and figure out what you would need to graduate."

We went through page by page, final grade by final grade. After consulting with his computer, and calling someone in the administration office, he hung up to share his findings.

"Well, not too bad, you only have to take three classes. A computer class, an English class, and a sociology class."

Only three classes! As is human nature, I overthought the task of returning to college, and in my mind had made it seem almost insurmountable. In my head, I had created a monster that didn't exist. Why do we do this to ourselves? It was not nearly as daunting as I had made it out to be. To quote Mark Twain, "I've had a lot of worries in my life, most of which never happened." I was unable to hide the big, silly grin on my face.

"I'm in! Let's do this!" I said.

Less than an hour later, I was again a student at Onondaga Community College. I had my class schedule, my student ID, my parking pass, and would soon have my textbooks. I took some time to walk around the campus again after all these years to reacquaint myself with the older buildings and get to know the newer ones. Once again, I had said yes to something life was offering up, and again that decision would lead to another memorable adventure.

I was a 55-year-old, second-semester sophomore, and therefore considered a "non-traditional" student, meaning I would be sitting next to students who were roughly the same age as my furnace. This was made painfully clear on the first day of my computer class when the instructor showed us a black and white picture of the original ENIAC electronic computer from 1946 on a PowerPoint slide show, and one of the young students turned to me and asked a simple question.

"Was that one hard to use?" he asked.

Let's see, in order for me to have been working on that computer in college in 1946, if I had been, say, 20 years old, I would have had to have been born in 1926. This was 2016. Apparently, to these kids, I appeared to be 90 years old.

On another occasion, the college was hosting an exhibit of United States presidential election memorabilia. It was an impressive collection of campaign buttons, posters, magazine covers, and newspaper articles. One of the very cool items was an original copy of the Chicago Daily Tribune newspaper from November 3rd of 1948, with the now-famous but inaccurate headline, "Dewey Defeats Truman." As I was admiring the rare framed newspaper, a young coed stopped to look at the Tribune display. After a moment or two, she turned and surprised me.

"Which one did you vote for?" she asked.

I thought for a moment and again quickly did the math in my head. In 1948, the legal voting age was 21, so if I had voted in that election, I would have had to have been born the same year the New York Yankees sent Babe Ruth up to bat third in the lineup, followed by Lou Gehrig as part of the legendary Murderers' Row in 1927. Many of the kids in the computer class were aware that I was still working in radio in Syracuse, and based on my interactions with them, they must have believed that I began my career reporting on the Hindenburg disaster. I told her that I voted for Truman.

I thoroughly enjoyed being around younger people while on campus. Occasionally, I would overhear conversations that just made me smile. For example, while in the campus bookstore, 2 guys were in line and noticed another guy's colorful, silk-screened T-shirt depicting a man's face. The first guy piped up.

"Wow, cool shirt. You hardly ever see him without a hat." His buddy answered with his own question.

"See who without a hat?"

"Zak Brown, the face on that shirt," the first guy replied, referring to the popular country star.

After a short pause, his buddy corrected his friend. "I'm pretty sure that's Aristotle on his shirt."

I turned my head to giggle under my breath. I was also pretty sure Aristotle would have liked his fried chicken and beer. I also believe he would have liked turning up the dial on the radio, as I imagine Aristotle was a typical guy who, despite living over two thousand years ago, liked to rock.

Another overheard conversation that brought a smile occurred while leaving a class and walking back to my car. Two coeds were in front of me near the Gordon Student Center when one of the girls offered up an observation.

"There aren't any cute guys here."

Her friend was ready with a response.

"My sister said guys don't get cute until they're 28. And then that's when we get ugly."

The first girl replied, sounding horrified.

"Oh. My. God. Is that true?!"

To which her friend admitted, "Maybe. But my sister drinks a lot, and she just got a cat."

I had so many fun, entertaining, and enlightening conversations with my younger classmates in that final semester at OCC. I think at some point every adult over the age of 40 should sign up for a class of some kind, not only for the educational value, but for the chance to interact with other students of different ages and diverse backgrounds. It's good for the mind and soul. And as much as I would laugh at some of the conversations, it also brought me back to my own memories of silly things my friends and I said and did when we were that age. It was a satisfying and, in many ways, a humbling experience returning to a college environment after all those years.

One of the experiences that I had missed when I left college in 1981 to start my career was walking across the stage at graduation and receiving my diploma. I graduated with my Associate's in Applied Sciences degree with my fellow classmates at Onondaga Community College on May 14th of 2016 at the age of 55. The walk was exciting and gratifying. You really are never too old to do anything. When the college president instructed us to move the tassel on our mortar boards from the right to the left to signify that we were now college graduates, I got emotional with a lump in my throat. I think in life we are often proud of our families, proud of our spouses, proud of our friendships and relationships, maybe even proud of our favorite sports teams. We sometimes forget that it's okay to be proud of ourselves. At that moment, college degree in hand, I was proud of myself. And it felt good.

I was glad to be finished, but I also knew that I would miss the students who provided me with so many great memories and laughs. Graduation day did not disappoint. As the graduates' names were being announced, the students who performed exceptionally well would have the phrase "Cum Laude" added after their degree, signifying excellence in their academic coursework. After several students' names were announced with the Cum Laude tag, a young coed sitting next to me during the ceremony turned to her friend and said with amazement, "Wow, that's like the 20th person with that last name. It must be an Indian thing."

CHAPTER 18

MY MUSICAL HIGHLIGHT REEL

E very now and then, you have a moment or an event that touches all of the emotions. In his famous "Don't ever give up" speech, the late North Carolina State legendary basketball coach Jim Valvano famously suggested that a full day should consist of laughing, thinking, and crying. Radio provided one of those moments for me in August of 2018.

All summer long, our radio station, TK99, had been promoting a fun concert at the local Lakeview Amphitheater with a great southern rock lineup. Old school favorite Hank Williams, Jr. would open the show, Marshall Tucker Band would follow, then the country rock sound of .38 Special, and the legendary Lynyrd Skynyrd would headline the concert. I had been fortunate to have seen all of these bands individually over the years, but never on the same bill. This was setting up to be a memorable night.

The Lakeview Amphitheater, known in Central New York as "The Amp," was one of those projects debated by politicians, made fun of by skeptics, and eventually built despite negative reviews, primarily from people who used to tell me to "get off my lawn." Admittedly, the Amp did go up pretty quickly, and the first few shows experienced some growing pains, but after all is said and done, it is a nice lakeside concert venue.

The night of the concert was a perfect night by Central New York standards, meaning clear skies and plenty of cold beer. Winters are long and often harsh in this part of the state, so when the warm weather of summer arrives, we really take full advantage of it and practically live outdoors. The parking lot of the Amp was filling up, and fans were tailgating, having some beers, tossing footballs, and blasting Skynyrd. We were having a big pre-concert broadcast for the radio station from the side of the stage, which was a treat because we could listen to the bands as they played songs for their sound checks.

It was all hands on deck, so our entire staff was there. My morning show co-host Lisa Chelenza, Alex "Bender" Conn, after-noon musicologist Rick DeYulio, program director and host of the popular Sunday morning show *The Blue Moon Cafe* Mimi Griswold, extreme engineer Tim Backer; Ralph Rotella, "The Shoe Repair Man;" and Big Wyatt, "America's Bouncer." We had a blast during the broadcast, getting hyped up for the show. This was as solid an air staff as I have ever worked with, and great people.

Hank started the concert playing a nice mix of his rocking tunes and some of his father's classics. I remembered those old songs from my youth, as my father was a fan of Hank Sr., and hear-ing them again brought me back to my youth. My dad had joined the old Columbia House record club, and a collection of Hank Sr. hits had arrived in the mail, so we heard those songs often.

For those who don't remember the Columbia House record club, it was an amazing concept where you joined the club, picked 10 albums, and paid just 99 cents, and they would mail the al-bums to your house. If you forgot to fill out the little card every month and mail it back, they would just automatically send you a random selection and charge you the regular price. This process would continue every month for the remainder of your life, as it was nearly impossible to cancel your membership to the Columbia

House record club. Basically, it was the same business model as today's streaming services. Honestly, it may have been easier to get out of the mob. I believe there are currently thousands of people living anonymously in the federal witness protection program for the sole purpose of hiding from the Columbia House record club.

Marshall Tucker Band followed Hank, and they did not disappoint. Their mix of country, blues, and a touch of jazz sounded great on a perfect summer evening. The southern rock band had been around since 1972, and had just one original member, but the seasoned musicians were tight, and the crowd knew every lyric to every song. In this day and age of recorded backing vocals and lip syncing, I still appreciate an artist or band that goes out there playing and singing their own music, even if it no longer sounds perfect. Doug Gray is the last original member of The Marshall Tucker Band, and while he may not be able to hit all the high notes like he once did, his presence and heart are still undeniable. You can not watch him and hear him without smiling. Listening to their hit "Can't You See" brought back the memory of a friend trying to learn to play that song on a guitar for the sole purpose of meeting a girl on the school bus.

The southern rock continued with .38 Special. The veteran band out of Jacksonville, Florida, sounded as good as they did decades before, and I sang along with the crowd as they played their many blues-based classic tunes. Their 1982 album *Special Forces* was the first album I ever brought home from a radio station, a gift from my stint at WRMV in Herkimer.

After a brief break for the roadies to set up, the lights dimmed, the crowd rose to its feet, and the voice of the backstage announcer filled the Amphitheater with their famous introduction.

"Ladies and gentlemen, please welcome Rock and Roll Hall of Fame band, Lynyrd Skynyrd!"

From the start to the end of their set, few fans sat down. One iconic song after another, effortlessly performed by the well-traveled southern rock legends. I'm sure they've played these songs at every concert, city after city, mile after mile, and year after year for decades. If they were tired or bored, they didn't show it. They played every song as if they were making musical magic for the very first time, with the enthusiasm of young, hungry musicians just starting out. I am neither a musician nor a music critic; I just enjoy live music with a few beers. To my ears, it was a great concert.

I have been to hundreds of concerts and performances of all kinds, from fraternity house garage bands to bar bands to performances on cruise ships, to stadium and arena concerts, you name it. I would guess that, at somewhere around 99.9% of these live performances, someone has randomly yelled out to the band, "Play Freebird!" For the first time ever, at least for me, the band played it. Those opening chords and notes are among the most recognizable in all of music. And I sang every lyric along with the 16 thousand-plus fans that night. It was nothing short of fantastic. It was emotional as I realized this would probably be the last time I would ever hear "Freebird" played LIVE by Lynyrd Skynyrd as the band was on its farewell tour, and no one is getting any younger. That Friday night summer concert in August of 2018 was literally the early part of my life set to music. I felt honored to be there.

The next day, the Marcellus High School class of 1978 got together for our 40th reunion at beautiful Marcellus Park. The late, legendary comedian George Burns once said, "Be careful, the first hundred years go by pretty quick." He wasn't wrong. While I hope to make it to a hundred, I'm not quite there yet, so I can't speak to that number. But I can tell you that the 40 years between high school graduation and that Saturday afternoon reunion went by in the blink of an eye. My former classmates and I shared so many great stories of practical jokes and pranks, some involving firecrackers and the principal's Volkswagen. Those of us who grew up in that era would agree that we were fortunate that cell phone cameras and YouTube had not yet been invented, as most of us would be unemployable as adults. Great times and memories.

That weekend in August of 2018 provided perspective. Many of my friends from the class of 1978 are no longer with us, providing further evidence that time remains undefeated. Time always wins. That weekend gave me permission to move forward, a reminder that it's okay to leave some things behind. After all, you can't accept new gifts if your hands are still holding the old ones. It's okay to put some of them down now. Much of that summer weekend was like watching a movie of my life. And I liked it. A lot.

CHAPTER 19

PHELPS AND THE THREE-LEGGED DOG

I have always enjoyed traveling. My great-grandfather was a railroad man, a conductor on trains in the eastern and northern parts of New York State. My aunt once told me that he worked on the trains until he retired in his seventies, then continued to wake up in the morning, make a sandwich, and head down to the railyard to sit and watch trains. I have also admired people with that kind of passion. She also told me that when my dad returned from the Korean War in 1957, she drove her late 1930s car from Saranac Lake to the train station in Utica to pick him up and bring him home to the north country. We have heard family stories of distant relatives who ran a riverboat up on the Hudson River to northern New York and Vermont. My brother Gregg spent 37 years as a commercial airline pilot. I absolutely love to drive. Anytime, anywhere. I suppose it's in the blood.

I also love to visit the unique parts of Americana that many others like to avoid. Anyone who has driven up and down the East Coast on I-95 or the old 301 has invariably driven past the over-the-top tourist destination known as "South of the Border." Signs for this hotel, located in South Carolina, just "south of the border" from North Carolina, begin showing up pretty much at the end of your driveway, regardless of your starting point. Even if you had not planned on stopping at South of the Border, by the time you get near it, you want to swing in for a look, and perhaps buy a classic bumper sticker. It's good old-fashioned Americana at its finest.

Every state has destinations like this. For example, when traveling to South Dakota, many tourists choose to visit Mount Rushmore. I, on the other hand, would prefer to see the 40-foot-tall wooden Jackalope in the town of Wall. When visiting Arizona, most people like to see the Grand Canyon, and maybe stay at the El Tovar hotel on the South Rim of the canyon. When my road trip friend Tom and I visited the Grand Canyon state, we wanted to stand on a corner in Winslow, just like in the classic song "Take It Easy" by The Eagles. For the record, there was no girl in a pickup truck, and no one hit their brakes to look at us. (However, there was a female mannequin sitting up in a flatbed Ford, permanently set up in a parking spot across the street for the benefit of tourists like us.) Instead of the El Tovar hotel, we preferred to stay at the famous Route 66 Wigwam Village Motel in Holbrook. To each his own.

New York State has many such attractions. You could go to Manhattan and stand in line to visit the Statue of Liberty, or go to the Port Authority Bus Terminal, stand in no line, and see the Statue of Jackie Gleason's bus-driving character from *The Honeymooners*, Ralph Cramden. It really is quite impressive.

About an hour or so west of Syracuse is the beautiful Finger Lakes Region of New York State, a unique area complete with picturesque lakes, dozens of wineries, and stores selling Amish-made furniture. The Finger Lakes were formed 2 million years ago by glaciers, and when they receded north, they left behind beautiful scenery, and the perfect terrain to grow wine-making grapes, which led to the arrival of countless busloads of bachelorette parties.

There is also much history in this part of the state. For example, the cute little town of Bedford Falls depicted in the classic holiday movie *It's A Wonderful Life* was supposedly based on the real village of Seneca Falls. There are also other, older villages in the area that look as though they were fashioned after Bedford Falls had George Bailey not been born. There is a little bit of everything in the Finger Lakes.

About 20 minutes to the west of Seneca Falls lies the Finger Lakes town of Phelps, known for its annual sauerkraut festival held every August. That may explain another famous Phelps landmark, one of the few remaining two-story outhouses in America. This is true. And the fact that it is connected to the main house on two floors, and that each floor has a three-seater, makes this a truly one-of-a-kind attraction. The two-story outhouse was built in 1869, and given there are no partitions between the drop holes, meant you had to be pretty good friends to all go in there and have a seat.

My friend Tom was visiting his dad in Buffalo, and when he called to ask if I wanted to meet him halfway for lunch, I knew exactly where we had to go. And by go, I mean have lunch. We settled on an old school spot in Geneva called Beef and Brew. Tom and I always try to find and support local ma and pa restaurants and businesses on our travels. We met at noon, had some delicious sandwiches and a cold adult beverage of moderation, and then jumped into Tom's car for the 15-minute drive to Phelps.

The village of Phelps is typical of many of the small towns and villages in the northeast. There is an old main street that, while attractive and quaint, has seen better times, but also appears to be on the rebound. There are a couple of nice, older family restaurants, some shops, and a few empty storefronts flanking the three-corner intersection. On 66 Main Street, at the intersection of North Wayne Street, sits the Howe House, which consists of the Phelps Historical Society, the Carriage House, and the famous two-story outhouse.

The impressive brick structure is behind the main house, connected by those walkways. While the primary entrance to the Howe House and the rest of the property is on Main Street, it's actually easier to see the outhouse from North Wayne Street, which is what we did. It's always amazing to see what craftsmen were able to build with only the tools and techniques available at the time of construction. Moreover, it's intriguing to think of the guy who designed and built the house back in 1869. I can only imagine the conversation the home's owner, Dr. Howe, had with his wife.

"Honey, I'm tired of walking downstairs in the middle of the night, and then going outside to use the outhouse, and then walking back upstairs afterward. I'm taking the horse and carriage over to the Home Depot and talking to the guys about putting a second story on the outhouse. Next, I'm going to talk to an engineer about designing an elevated bridge walkway from our bedroom to the outhouse, and then hiring a plumber to figure out the best way to manage the flow from the second floor down to the first floor. Then, I'll head over to the bank to take out a home equity loan, and possibly cash out some of my 401(k) money to pay for it all. I can't see any other way of doing what I want done," to which Mrs. Howe probably responded, "Why don't we just sleep in the downstairs bedroom?"

Since men have not been listening to their wives since the beginning of time, Dr. Howe went ahead and built his amazing two-story outhouse. It really is something that fascinates guys. For example, we get excited when we check into a hotel room and discover there is a working telephone right next to the toilet. Women ask, "Who would ever use a phone that is right next to a toilet?" to which men reply, "Honey, do you mind? I'm taking a call right now." When men see a two-story, three-seat-per-floor outhouse, we instantly want to sit on it and take it for a ride.

As it turned out, the Howe House was technically not open on the day we visited. After a brief moment of disappointment, we noticed a construction crew around the back of the main structure where the outhouse is located. We slowly started to stroll around the back toward the two-story outhouse, faking as if we were just a couple of dudes walking and possibly taking a shortcut back to

North Wayne Street. We were prepared with a solid excuse as to why we were going in that direction in the event someone stopped us to ask, "Where do you think you're going?" As luck would have it, the excuse was not needed as the workers were on a lunch break. Bingo.

The first floor of the outhouse was open, as that was where the repairs were taking place. The facility was just as advertised, a solid three-seater. There they were, "side-by-side-by-side" wooden outhouse toilets with no partitions between them. Even with my closest friends, I could not envision a situation where this would have been cool. I've had to leave hotel rooms shared with friends because of what was going on in the bathroom. I couldn't imagine a scenario that sounded like the setup to a joke. "So, three guys go into a three-seater outhouse together..."

But what did we immediately want to do as soon as we went into the structure? "Quick, Tom, let me take a picture of you sitting on the wooden outhouse hole, and then you take my picture. Make it look like you're struggling." I snapped a couple of quick two-story outhouse pictures, and then we switched with Tom getting a couple of nice shots of me on the historic wooden toilet seat. Mission accomplished.

After a few more minutes of admiring the architecture and brilliant design of the structure, we headed back out to the sidewalk and into the downtown business district of Phelps. Again, as with many of the towns and villages of the Rust Belt, there was a combination of cute restaurants, a few shops, and a few vacant storefronts. We walked on the sidewalk through the one main intersection of town, not really seeing many people at all. We stopped a few times to take pictures, and as we continued down the sidewalk, we spotted a guy walking a dog on a leash headed in our direction on the same side of the sidewalk. It was definitely not a purebred dog, just a good old mixed-breed lovable mutt. As we approached the guy and his dog, it became obvious that the dog was struggling to walk in a straight line, stumbling a little with every other step.

As we all met on the sidewalk coming from opposite directions, the reason for the dog's stumbling became clear. The poor thing was navigating on only three legs. To be exact, on a car, it would have been the passenger side, front wheel that was missing. Tom and I felt bad for the little fellow. It was hard not to. He was plugging along, doing the best he could do. As we walked by, I squatted down to pet the little guy and offer canine words of encouragement to him. (Here is the public service announcement part of this story. Never pet a strange dog, no matter how cute it is.) Just when I reached over to pet him on the head, he stopped his hobbling, jumped up on his two healthy hind legs, and bit me on my left forearm.

Fortunately, I was wearing my old green fall jacket that was also on its final legs. Although it was a sturdy coat, it had seen its better days. In fact, my wife had condemned the coat to the thrift store after it was admired and complimented by a homeless gentleman in downtown Syracuse while on our way to dinner one evening, offering me a solid fist-bump as we passed each other to celebrate our similar taste in fashion. When we returned home, my green jacket was put in a pile meant for donations. I secretly rescued my favorite coat from the thrift store bag and hid it in the back of the closet next to another coat of mine that I realized I had not worn in almost four years. The green jacket would be safe there.

The now vicious three-legged dog growled as his jaws closed on my left forearm, protected by the thickness of my green jacket. I yelled, "WHOA!" as I jumped back up from my crouched position. The dog retreated as his owner calmed him down.

"Are you ok?!" Tom asked with concern. I took a close look, and other than some teeth marks on my jacket, there appeared to be no further damage. Mainly, there was no blood.

"What the hell was that?" Tom asked. "You just got bit by a three-legged dog!" I thought about it for a moment, and then realized I may have just made history.

"Think about it. I just took a seat on a rare, two-story outhouse wooden toilet seat, and then, less than 10 minutes later, was bitten by a three-legged dog. I'm willing to bet anything that up until that very moment, that had never happened before in the history of mankind."

Neither Tom nor I partake in now-legal marijuana, but if we did, that would have been the perfect moment to smoke the devil's lettuce and further discuss the "two-story outhouse, three-legged dog bite theory" on a deeper level. However, we do enjoy beer. All these years, and beers, later, and we still have not reached any solid conclusions. But it is still fun to talk about.

CHAPTER 20

RADIO CALLERS

As on-air radio personalities, we sometimes forget that people really are listening to what we have to say and that our stories and conversations impact their lives. At its core, radio has always been a people business. Unfortunately, as broadcasters, we sometimes forget that.

Every radio DJ has one very common shared experience. It doesn't matter if you crack the microphone in Omaha, Herkimer, El Paso, Bakersfield, or New York City; every radio station has its regular phone callers who can be funny, entertaining, quite possibly annoying, but always memorable. My first radio job was at 1420AM, WRMV, "Radio of the Mohawk Valley" in Herkimer, New York. I don't mean to brag, but every two weeks I took home $214.00. The rent for my little apartment on King Street was $190 per month, including utilities. My student loan payment was $46.32, and my health insurance was $88 per month. Fortunately, my 1973 Ford Gran Torino was paid for. I was still responsible for the car insurance, groceries, and a Sunday night dinner at Ponderosa Steakhouse, a few beers at the Palmer House on Main Street, and other general living expenses. There was little left at the end of the month, but I was on my own and paying my bills

I had an odd schedule at WRMV. My work week was Friday

through Tuesday, so my regular days off were Wednesdays and Thursdays. My parents still lived just west of Syracuse in Marcellus, and I made the 1-hour and 45-minute drive every other week or so. There were times when I was literally down to my last dollar or so. I took the New York State Thruway, and on more than one occasion, I had to get off at the Canastota exit because I only had 90 cents on me. The cost of the toll to Syracuse was $1.35. On a positive note, the route to Marcellus from Canastota went through the village of Manlius, where a bar called Buffoons had free chicken wings on Wednesdays. Boom.

Most of the on-air people I have worked with over the years in this crazy business have similar stories. We're one step away from being circus people, working odd hours and crazy weekend shifts for peanuts. I spent the first few years in broadcasting basically broke, but I was having a blast. Radio people are passionate people who enjoy the spotlight of being on the air and the occasional free food that shows up at the radio station. We are like theater people, but with a slightly better credit score.

Many of my fondest memories of my younger days are the times I spent with my coworkers. There was a time when a legitimate social option was to go hang out at the radio station. That speaks to the fun of the job. Off the top of my head, I can't think of many other jobs where, on your days off, you want to go back to the job and just hang out. Often, I would just hang out in the studio with whoever was on the air at the time and answer the request line. Listeners and callers are the lifeblood of a radio station, and the request line was a direct line to the voice on the radio.

My first regular caller at the radio station in Herkimer was a guy from the small town of Dolgeville who called himself "Buffalo Bill," long before the character from the classic movie *The Silence of the Lambs*. Bill called me every day at around 6:00 PM just to say "hi." I still have one of the handwritten messages from the receptionist that I had missed a call from him.

Overnight radio was a great place to hone your communication skills, and by that, I mean talk to girls on the request line. I know plenty of guys who went out on dates with girls they met on the request line, even one guy who met his wife that way. Personally, I never had much luck meeting girls on the request line. In one instance, while doing the overnight show on Y94 in Syracuse in the mid-1980s, after talking to a lovely-sounding girl named Jennifer on the phone almost every night for several weeks, I suggested we meet up sometime. She instantly became very excited.

"Yes, that would be great," she replied. The next sentence, however, was the deal breaker.

"Could we meet after the holidays? I'm scheduled to be released by then."

"Um, why don't you give me a call when you get out; maybe we could get a coffee or something," is all I could muster up to say in response.

Jennifer never did call after the holidays that year; perhaps she was not granted the release she was counting on. But it is an example of the connection listeners experience with radio personalities. I never knew what facility she was scheduled to be released from, or what happened that brought that situation in her life. She had access to a radio, and for whatever reason, felt a connection to me such that she picked up the phone and wanted to chat.

Sadly, there are very few live overnight or weekend airshifts anymore, with those time slots replaced by the technology of voice tracking or satellite-delivered programming. Having worked nighttime and overnight radio for many years at the start of my career, I spoke with hundreds, if not thousands, of listeners on the request line. Most were just calling to say hi or to make a song request. Many were just lonely and simply calling to talk to someone. I suppose all those lonely souls turned to social media for company late at night after those jobs were eliminated and there was no longer anyone answering the phone. Radio truly was the first social media

One of my favorite regular callers was a young guy named

Donnie who called every night for almost two years that I did overnights on Y94 in Syracuse. He called from a local psychiatric hospital where he was a resident. Donnie was only 24 years old and had been living at the hospital for two years. He was always in a great mood when he called and was a great conversationalist. He would start right up as soon as I answered the request line.

"Hi, Y94FM."

"Hey Gomez, do you like Paul McCartney?" Donnie was already excited.

"I sure do, Donnie, he's a legend."

"Good," Donnie whispered. "Because he's listening right now."

One night, the request line was blinking with an incoming call, and I hit the button to answer the phone.

"Hi, Y94FM."

"Hey, Gomez, I quit smoking today," Donnie exclaimed.

"Why today?" I asked.

"Because Peter Gabriel told me to."

It took me a while, but I finally figured out that Donnie was taking much of his life advice from song lyrics. The line, "kick the habit," is from Peter Gabriel's song "Sledgehammer." He would also incorporate movie dialogue into his conversations, either knowingly or unknowingly. At the time, I assumed this was part of the reason he was living at the psychiatric hospital.

"Hey, Gomez, there are four girls named Lisa on my floor right now, two nurses and two patients."

"What do you think that means, Donnie?" I asked.

"Beware of the dwarf," a reference from the movie *Foul Play*. I have no idea what he meant by that, but I still remember it all these years later. I always liked talking to Donnie and often wondered what became of him and if he ever made it out of the psychiatric facility. He was refreshing and funny, and said whatever was on his mind. The world could use more Donnies.

Another regular caller from Central New York was a young lady from East Syracuse who would call our show on TK99 almost every

175

morning for a good year and a half or more, and offer up way too much personal information on the air.

"Good morning, TK99," we said, answering the request line.

"I'm really happy today," she would declare.

"Why is that?" we responded.

"My STD test came back negative."

This admission was followed by more information we didn't necessarily need, TMI.

"I'm going out to buy a new swimsuit today. Do you know if two-piece suits come in size 26?"

Once again, for whatever reason, she felt a connection so strong with our show that she wanted to tell us very personal things about her life. I think people who are completely unafraid to share anything and everything about themselves are among the most interesting people on the planet.

In the mid-1990s, our morning show based on TK99 in Syracuse was also simulcast into the Utica, New York, market on WRCK, Rock 107. The 50 thousand watt signal boomed throughout the Mohawk Valley and into the Adirondack Mountains. A guy started calling our show every morning from his cabin way up in the Central Adirondacks, a good 90 minutes or so north of Utica. He called himself "Napalm," a nickname from his stint in the Army during the Vietnam War. Napalm would randomly call and do things like place his cordless phone into an empty 55-gallon drum out behind his cabin in the woods, and then shoot different guns at the barrel so we could hear the difference between the various rifles, pistols, and ammunition. It was more fascinating than it sounds.

One Saturday afternoon in the fall of that year, my morning show partner, Dave, and I were at a record store in the Utica suburb of New Hartford for a radio station appearance when a big Harley-Davidson motorcycle pulled up. The rider dismounted from the impressive bike, removed his helmet, and walked into the record store to say hi. This was when we met Napalm in person. He was as friendly a guy as I have ever met. He stayed and chatted for a few minutes, and we had a few laughs. As he turned to leave the store to head back to his mountain cabin, he left us with this thought.

"It's about a 90-mile trip to get here on my Harley. This is the farthest I have been away from my cabin since I got back from 'Nam."

As he waved and left the store, I realized this may have been the biggest compliment from a listener I had ever received. Napalm made such a strong connection over the airwaves with our show that he felt compelled to ride his motorcycle farther than he had in decades to put faces to the voices that he had been listening to. I will never forget the passion of the man nicknamed "Napalm."

Then there was "Razor," who called regularly for a few years until he decided to stop paying his phone bill. Razor was most famous with our listeners as the guy who called one morning, and LIVE on the air, attached a battery charger to his testicles. According to his wife, who was assisting him, "There were sparks, and a little bit of smoke." It was truly epic morning radio.

Every now and then, the request line would light up right at 6:00 in the morning, just as we were starting the show. More often than not, a young woman named Lisa was on the other end of the line, just returning from work. Lisa was a professional escort who would freely offer up details about her clients from the night before, especially if there had been a big conference or sports event in town. To speak with her, you would not have guessed that she was a fan of classic rock, but she knew a lot of the music. Specifically, Lisa took much of her life advice from The Eagles' song, "Already Gone," and she would often weave lyrics from that great tune into her conversation. The part of the song that spoke to her was the lyrics that suggest how to find the key to unlock the chains we often find ourselves living in. Great song, superb lyrics, funny lady. I have always hoped that she found her key and is living a good life.

Perhaps the most popular of the regular phone callers was the legendary "Elvis Mike," the world's biggest Elvis fan. Anytime Mike

177

called from his house, there was an Elvis Presley movie playing on his VCR. And I mean 24/7. Non-stop Elvis at Mike's house.

Mike called the radio show regularly for several years, selflessly sharing countless stories of trips to Canadian casinos, Graceland in Memphis, and Las Vegas. In fact, he told us on the air that he had met his significant other at a casino, as she was the blackjack dealer at his table. Within a week, she was living with him, and then he took her to Vegas, where he bribed a bellhop to show them the room at the Riviera Hotel where Elvis and Priscilla were married. Elvis Mike certainly took a big bite out of life.

One day, several years ago, a box was delivered to the radio station containing only Elvis sunglasses, fake sideburns, and cheap silk scarves. There was no note or any other explanation. The next morning, Mike called on the air and asked if we had received the package.

"Yes, we did," I said. "But there was no card, or note, or anything."

Mike responded in his very distinct Central New York accent. "Someday when I die, I want youse guys to wear those items when youse bury me at Sonnenburg Gardens in Canandaigua."

As nice as that sounded, burial at Sonnenburg Gardens would have been difficult, as the facility is a beautiful residence, and the digging of a grave in the public garden would have been frowned upon. And illegal. Still, it was Elvis Mike's favorite place on earth, and we told him the same thing DJs often tell listeners who call with specific song requests.

"We'll see what we can do."

Years came and went, and eventually we stopped hearing from Elvis Mike, mainly because he had met a wonderful Amish girl, became Amish himself, and lived a simple Amish lifestyle. I have no idea how that all came about, but I'm absolutely sure it must have been an awesome story. The simple Amish lifestyle does not involve many phone calls, so I really don't know much about it beyond our last conversation with him.

One morning during the radio show, a relative of Mike's called us off the air to tell us that Mike had passed away a few days earlier. I am positively sure that Mike died a happy man, and he certainly had fun along the journey. We looked forward to his daily updates, and they never failed to entertain. Mike was another great listener who found connection with radio and our show. He was comfortable enough to call and share almost every part of his life with us, and our other listeners.

Obviously, Elvis Mike would not be buried at Sonnenburg Gardens. His cousin told us he was not cremated, so there would be no chance of bringing some of his ashes to spread somewhere on the property, which I assume is also frowned upon. While cleaning out the radio studio in the spring of 2021, I found some of the many Elvis trinkets, including some of the ones he bought from me, that Mike had given us over the years. There were also the Elvis sunglasses, the fake sideburns, and the silk scarves. I brought the other small items home. It is about 71 miles from my house to Sonnenburg Gardens. If you visit, you might find a small picture of Elvis behind some beautiful flowers. Rest in peace, Elvis Mike.

SIGNING OFF

I have had the good fortune to have worked with so many amazing broadcasters throughout my career, now spanning five decades. The radio business attracts talent from a wide variety of backgrounds, some requiring weekly drug tests. As long as you have a story to tell, radio will find a place for you. I have worked with everyone from people who have advanced college degrees from prestigious universities, to someone who attended the Ringling Brothers Clown College in Florida. I have also worked with a guy who is no longer allowed to reside in New Jersey. He had some amazing stories.

We had an overnight DJ who, despite growing up and living in Syracuse his entire life, got lost on his way to work. He drove to the station every night for over two years, yet somehow that night he couldn't find it. He called me at home at 11:45 PM to ask me how to get to the radio station. I don't know what happened to him, and there is a good chance neither does he.

We had an intern from one of the local colleges who showed up on his first day, clogged the only toilet in the building, drove to a hardware store to buy a plunger, unclogged the toilet, and then drove back to campus and changed his major. Smart move.

I have also worked with broadcasters who went on to big-time, major network positions. I was in Nashville for an Arthritis Foundation Telethon with our television crew from WTVH-TV5, the local CBS affiliate in Syracuse. I was one of the hosts of the annual broadcast, along with Channel 5 reporter Liz Ayers, and the great sports anchor and host Mike Tirico, who began his amazing television career at WTVH and was the sports director at the time. Mike was my roommate for the few days in Nashville, and we had a blast. Mike and I went to the Grand Ole Opry, and were treated to the very first appearance on the legendary Opry stage of a young up-and-comer named Garth Brooks. I was sitting next to Mike as Garth came out onstage. Garth played his first single, "If Tomorrow Never Comes," and he sounded good. When he finished, he humbly tipped his cowboy hat to the crowd's gracious applause and left the stage. I remember turning to Mike and whispering, "He seems like a nice guy, but I don't see him going anywhere." That is why I am not in the music business.

One of the most talented people I have ever worked with in radio was Phil Markert. Phil was an iconic mainstay in Syracuse radio and television for the better part of fifty years, and he was an old-school entertainer. He was an amazing piano player, a great broadcaster, and an accomplished actor. Not only did Phil appear in dozens of local theater productions over the years, but he was also in two Hollywood movies: *Blue Velvet*, starring Isabella Rossellini, and *Marie*, starring Sissy Spacek and Morgan Freeman. He was also in an episode of *Unsolved Mysteries* playing the part of a murder victim. There are probably enough Phil Markert stories to fill its own book.

Many years ago, Phil came out to watch one of my comedy shows at a Syracuse venue called Jazz Central. Phil just enjoyed any and all LIVE performances. We were chatting after the show, and Phil asked, "Hey, do you want to go over to Daisy Dukes? My granddaughter is working there tonight, and at 11:00, they all get on the bar and do a line dance." Daisy Dukes was a popular country-music-themed bar in Armory Square, not far from Jazz Central.

"Absolutely," I said. It sounded like a great way to top off the night.

We made the short drive to Daisy Dukes, and we somehow squeezed our way into the crowded, hopping night spot. I grabbed us two beers from the bar, and as we waited for the 11:00 line dance, I noticed a group of college-aged girls looking in our direction. I gave Phil a nudge.

"Phil, look over there. I think those girls are looking at you," as I nodded in their direction.

"Nah," Phil replied. "They're probably looking at you. I could be their grandfather." He wasn't wrong. Phil had been a broadcast legend in Syracuse for more than double their age.

"I don't know," I continued. "Come on, Phil, you are famous in this town. They might recognize you from the radio, TV, or theater." Even as Phil shook his head, one of the young ladies smiled at Phil and gave him a little wave.

"See!" I blurted out. "She IS looking at you." It looked as though she was pointing Phil out to her friends, and maybe telling them who he was. It was like I was standing next to Brad Pitt, and the paparazzi had spotted him.

Suddenly, the first girl who had apparently recognized Phil and waved at him started making her way through the crowd. She came right up to us, said hi, and then spoke directly to Phil, and asked him for an autograph.

"Could you please sign this napkin for me?" she asked.

Phil was briefly stunned, and then said, "Why certainly. I don't have a pen or anything to write with."

"I have one right here, in my purse," she responded. She located it and handed it to Phil.

Phil was genuinely flattered, even a little flustered. He took the pen and the napkin and thought for a moment.

"Who do you want me to sign it to?" he asked the coed.

"Excuse me?" she replied.

"Well, is this for your mother or your aunt or somebody?" Phil asked. He assumed the girl was getting Phil's autograph as a surprise for one of her older family members.

"Oh, no, it's just for me," she answered. Phil smiled a big old-guy smile.

"So what's your name so I can personalize it for you?" he asked.

"Oh, I don't need anything personalized. You can just put your name."

"Well, okay," Phil said. Then he signed his name on the napkin and handed it back to her. Still a little baffled, Phil asked, "So do you listen to me on the radio?" She seemed surprised.

"You're on the radio? I didn't know that. That's cool!" she excitedly responded.

"I don't get it," Phil said. "If you didn't know me from the radio, and had no idea who I am, why did you want my autograph?"

"I'm here doing a scavenger hunt with a bachelorette party, and I had to get the signature of the oldest person in the bar." She smiled and then returned to her friends.

I laughed out loud. I mean, that was hysterical. The only person laughing harder than me was Phil. I am still grateful to have had that night out with him.

There are so many stories like that one, I could go on.... Oh, hang on a moment, the phone is ringing.

"Hi, you're caller number 8, please try again." To be continued...

ACKNOWLEDGEMENTS

Everybody has a favorite restaurant. While it's nice to occasion-ally go out to a fancy or upscale place for that experience of a special event, I can almost guarantee that most people have their favorite diner or neighborhood establishment to enjoy a comfortable, home-cooked meal and atmosphere. That is how I have approached every radio show that I have been a part of. My shows have never been the expensive steakhouse or trendy, glitzy restaurant. It has always been more of the local diner that has become a community center where you can enjoy some good, reliable comfort food, bump into old friends, and maybe meet some new ones. Many of those fancy restaurants have come and gone, but your favorite diner has been there as long as you can remember.

Throughout my 40-plus years behind the microphone, I have been blessed to work with many great broadcasters, many of whom became lifelong friends who still meet me at local diners for break-fast. It would be impossible to name them all. Between the on-air personalities and other radio station personnel, the number would be in the several hundreds, if not more.

Our staff at WKFM, not including the mice and snakes, was a fun group of guys. Brian Richards, Gary Dunes, and PD John Carucci provided a great, old-school radio atmosphere in which to learn. Jim Reith, who filled in and would later host a successful afternoon talk show on WSYR-AM, was always a solid broadcaster. And Brian Rubenau was, and still is, a reliable fill-in radio host.

The entire staff at Y94FM and WSYR was a stellar group of broadcasters, top to bottom. Many former co-workers from both successful radio stations went on to work at major markets and, in some cases, major network positions. "Dr." Phil Locasio was the afternoon host on Y94 and program director who hired me as a part-timer in 1984. "Big Mike's" Billboard Magazine award-winning "Y Morning Big Show" was just that. A big, fun, entertaining morning radio show. It would have been successful in almost any market. I was thrilled to have been a part of that show. The morning show consisted of Big Mike Fiss, the late Dick Deline, Dennis Brogan, aka the "Dome Ranger," "Traffic Tom" Paleveda, Marti Casper, Jeff Day, "Driver Don" Keaney, Dee Collins, and myself. What a great run on that show and that station.

The newsroom staff of WSYR was of major market quality, both in talent and character. I was honored to have worked with so many CNY broadcast legends at that facility, including the late Don Dauer. Don was a noted outdoorsman and would routinely do his last on-air morning radio break while wearing his hip waders to go fishing immediately after leaving the studio. Rick Gary was the Rick of the "Rick and Ron" show I listened to on the school bus as a teenager. It was a thrill to work with him at WSYR, and down the hall from TK99 on SUNNY 102.1.

Under John Butler's tutelage, the newsroom was a well-oiled machine, stacked with veteran anchors and talented reporters. The late Dave White was a great news writer and anchor, and we remained great friends for many years. We went on countless camping trips to the Adirondack Mountains for the better part of 25 years, numerous hockey games in Canada, and golf outings throughout the area. I miss his storytelling and laughter. Tom Langmyer was the Operations Manager and had a big hand in the success of both legendary radio stations. Obviously, Tom has remained a great friend and road trip companion for decades.

He also read an early draft of this book and provided some great insight.

Dick Ferguson was the President and CEO of NewCity Communications, the parent company of WSYR and Y94, for most of the years that I worked there. At a time when there were countless horror stories of radio station owners running sketchy operations, Dick was at the helm of perhaps the best radio group in America at the time. Broadcasters did, and still do, praise NewCity as a model for other broadcast companies to emulate. I learned so much about radio from him and his company during those formative years.

I have been hosting the morning show at WTKW since 1994. During the 30-plus years at classic rock TK99, I have had the absolute pleasure to work alongside some amazing broadcasters and good people. New York State Broadcasters Association Hall of Famer Mimi Griswold guided the station for most of those years, and co-hosted the morning with me for several years as well. Under her direction, the station moved the needle and prospered. For almost 20 years, the "Gomez and Dave" show anchored the radio station. My talented partner, Dave Coombs, and I enjoyed success for most of those years, and enjoyed many rounds of golf in tournaments around CNY. One of the great annual traditions with Dave, and future morning show co-host Lisa Chelenza, was broadcasting from the Big East college basketball tournaments in Manhattan every March, and watching Syracuse play in great games at Madison Square Garden, including the epic six overtime win over Connecticut in 2009. We had some truly memorable broadcasts from NYC during that run.

Other TK99 staff members include current afternoon jock and resident musicologist Rick Deyulio, midday host/program director Alex "Bender" Conn, and my current morning show co-host and longtime colleague Lisa Chelenza. They are all consummate radio professionals and just good people. Former WSYR-TV news personality TeNesha Murphy was a great co-host for a couple of years.

And the talented guys down the hall on our sister station, K-Rock, Josh and Cody in the morning, Smoothie, and program director Marissa Greenlar. From the sports side of the building, Paulie Scibilia has always been fun to work with. Carrie Wojtasek and her incredible events staff are among the hardest-working people in the building. None of this would be possible without the help and expertise of "Extreme Engineer" Tim Backer.

I always tell people that I am glad I don't have to compete against Ed Levine. Ed is the owner and CEO of Galaxy Media Partners. He is as sharp a radio guy as I have ever known. And definitely the most competitive. He has navigated the radio waters from an on-air jock to corporate program director and group owner. He and his wife, Pam, have grown a successful broadcast, events, and digital media company from the ground up, and it is a privilege to work for them at Galaxy.

I have also worked with many talented broadcasters who began as our morning show producers. A few that come to mind include Mike Pollock, "Kidd" Chris Foley, Jason "Fuzz" Fava, Michael "Doobie" McDonald, Steven Rogers, and Joe Salzone. We've had both a "Skeeter" and a "Scooter." We had Jordan Prietti, aka "Johnny Flop." Many of these guys have gone on to great success in radio, comedy, and voice acting. They're all great guys. I am sure that I am missing a few names on this list of current and former colleagues.

Morning radio shows have always enjoyed the college students who have spent time as interns. We have had so many over the years that I can only recall a few of their names. Sometimes, I will remember their morning show nickname. Occasionally, I'll bump into someone who will introduce themselves and say they were an intern years ago. I often just take their word for it. Thank you to the many interns who did everything from letting guests into the studio to screening phone calls to making coffee, and to just showing up. We've also had interns who did everything from racing each other in their underwear to eating dirt that had been microwaved.

We had an intern who painted a picture with his butt, and another who went to a wellness center and took an enema while on the phone with us.

I would also like to congratulate all of the callers on the various studio contest lines who have called my radio shows over the past 40-plus years, and won everything from concert tickets to Christmas trees to trips, and everything else we have given away over the past 4 decades. Radio stations have traditionally asked for "caller number 9" to win the prizes. In my 10 years at Y94 and my over 30 years at TK99, the incoming phone system has had three incoming lines. The first line is the actual studio number we give out over the air for contests, the other two are rollover lines. When we say "caller number 9 will win the concert tickets," we answer the lines and count up to nine. For example, "You're caller number one, please try again, you're caller number two, please try again," and so on until we get to "caller number nine," the winner.

Maybe it's just me, but over the years, I have noticed that the listeners who heard "You're caller number seven, please try again," seemed to be the most frustrated, often letting out the most audible sound of disappointment. My theory is that listeners who often call the station to win prizes have figured out the three-line phone system, and therefore know that if they are callers one through six, they still have a chance. But if they are the dreaded caller number seven, they have virtually no chance of being caller number nine. Therefore, I partially dedicate this book to anyone who has ever been caller number 7.

My wife, Kim, has always been my biggest supporter. She kept encouraging me to finish writing this book, and she read the very first draft of it, correcting the early grammar mistakes and spelling errors. She is a good writer and editor, and makes the best sauce in Central New York.

This book would not have been possible without the help and support of Laura Thorne and Jess Neiding from Wildebeest

Publishing. Their amazing team provided so much help and guidance.

Finally, a shout-out to all of the listeners. There have been thousands, and you all made my days memorable. Thank you for allowing me to hang out with you over the airwaves for over 40 years. Morning radio personalities are often the first voice someone hears when their alarm wakes them up in the morning. Every now and then, I will bump into a longtime listener who will introduce themselves, and then recount a story or a joke they remembered from my radio show and how it somehow helped them get through a bad day. Often, it is a story, a joke, or quip I had forgotten about until that moment. Over the years, many listeners have felt so connected to us that they have called the radio show to share their personal triumphs, and losses. Those are the moments that remind me of why I have enjoyed this crazy business for all of these years.

Thank you for listening for all of these years! So long for now.

My first day on the air at TK99. Joey Gates showing me the ropes.

Photo Credit: Steve Becker

The Turning Stone Resort and Casino … from left to right: Dave Coombs, Lisa Chelenza, me.

Photo Credit: coworker

At the Landmark Theater in Syracuse. Left to right: me, Dick Clark, Big Mike Fiss.

Photo Credit: Staff member

August 2018. The Lakeview Amphitheater in Syracuse. From left: Rick DeYulio, me, Big Wyatt Lozano, Mimi Griswold, Lisa Chelenza.

Photo Credit: Rick DeYulio

May 14, 2016. Onondaga Community College, SRC Arena. Getting my diploma.

Photo Credit: Fellow student, my phone/camera

Winter of 2017, Syracuse Marriott Downtown, me on the
left with Hall of Famer Coach Jim Boeheim.

Photo Credit: Rose Massett

October 27, 2022, at SRC Arena, Onondaga Community College.

Photo Credit: Guest using my phone/camera

July 2022, in the TK99 radio studio with Ralph Rotella, "the shoe repair man."

Photo Credit: selfie

October 20, 2018. With Phil Markert at North Syracuse Piano and Organ store.
Photo Credit: Guest using my phone/camera

WTVH-TV studios in Syracuse, April 1989. Hosting the telethon
with legendary sports broadcaster Mike Tirico.
Photo Credit: Staff member

195

ABOUT THE AUTHOR

Glenn Gomez Adams is an award-winning broadcast journalist and radio personality in Syracuse, New York. He has been acknowledged by the New York State Broadcasters Association numerous times and recognized by the Syracuse Press Club on several occasions, receiving multiple awards from both prestigious organizations. He is also a stand-up comedian and sought-after humorist, speaking and hosting events throughout the northeast.

When he is not behind the microphone or onstage, he can be found either behind his keyboard or behind the person in front of him at the Cracker Barrel. He is trying to teach his wife, Kim, to dance like Tatyana.

Connect with Glenn...
www.BaldGomez.com
Facebook: Gomez Adams
Instagram: instagomezgram

www.ingramcontent.com/pod-product-compliance
Lightning Source LLC
Chambersburg PA
CBHW020407150626
46554CB00012B/410